cooks' h

the art and soul of local, sustainable

D0117446

cooks' house

the art and soul of local, sustainable cuisine

Eric Patterson
and
Jennifer Blakeslee

PHOTOGRAPHY BY **THOMAS KACHADURIAN**

Spirituality
&Health
BOOKS

Spirituality
&Health
BOOKS

Spirituality & Health Books

129 ½ East Front Street

Traverse City, MI 49684

www.spiritualityhealthbooks.com

6/2011

Cover and interior design by Sandra Salamony

Cataloging-in-Publication data for this book
is available upon request.

ISBN: 978-0-9818708-2-3

Printed in China
First Printing, 2010

10 9 8 7 6 5 4 3 2

dedication

Eric:

To my mom who has always believed in me.
To my family who has supported me.
To Chef Dave Nelson who introduced me to my first love.

Jennifer:

To my daughter Abigail.

18 autumn

mesón mexicano

warm cactus & chorizo salad 21

chicken thighs braised in chocolate, chili peppers,
    dried cherries & stewed tomatoes 23

mother-in-law's flour tortillas 27

caramel flan 28

harvest celebration

mussel, white bean, kale & garlic soup 32

ragout of root vegetables & mushrooms 34

whole roasted beef tenderloin with wilted arugula
    & crushed fingerling potatoes 36

blue cheese cheesecake with pear compote 39

a menu for the melancholy

artichoke soup with walnuts & parsley 43

salad of roasted beets, beet greens & tatsoi
    with freshly grated ginger & chives 44

trout poached in miso broth
    with baby bok choy & burdock root 46

stewed plums with vanilla & muscat 49

late autumn

turnip soup with turnip greens & bacon 55

roast pheasant with cauliflower salad & bread sauce 58

warm indian creamed rice with pomegranates & pistachios 63

winter 64

christmas dinner

chestnut & oyster stew 67
salad of mâche, pomelo & christmas cactus flower 68
roast duck stuffed with onions & juniper berries,
     served with roasted turnips & apples 71
traditional plum pudding. 73

new year's eve

foie gras in brioche with pear compote. 76
velouté of sunchokes with hazelnuts & parsley 78
sautéed walleye with great lakes caviar & champagne sauce. 80
short ribs braised in red wine and star anise
     with potato purée & baby leeks 84
white & dark chocolate trifle 88

comfort food

classic french onion soup gratinée 94
roast chicken 96
braised winter greens 98
buttermilk biscuits with bacon & cheddar cheese. 99
dried fruit cobbler. 100

four of our favorite stews

daube of venison with mashed potatoes 104
cassoulet. 106
wild boar ragout with root vegetables,
     curly kale & cavatappi pasta. 110
braised veal cheeks with cabbage, raisins & potatoes 112

spring

hot and cold

COLD SPRING MENU

purée of jerusalem artichoke soup with garlic confit 119

roast quail on polenta with dried plums 120

greek walnut-honey cake with earl grey ice cream 122

WARM SPRING MENU

stinging nettle soup with horseradish dumplings 124

new potatoes & white anchovies with vinegar onions 126

chicken legs stuffed with sausage,
    served with porcini mushrooms & fava beans 129

tangerine mousse 132

easter

tatsoi & sorrel salad with pickled ramps, boiled eggs & tarragon 134

seven hour leg of lamb with fava beans, peas,
    savory & goat cheese gnocchi 137

peaches with cardamom & muscat 140

celebrating heirloom vegetables

salad of butter crunch, flame & paris white lettuces with
    tempura of fairy tale eggplant, upland cress,
    chrysanthemum flowers & french breakfast radishes 143

platter of grilled bianca di maggio onions, fresh sardines,
    swedish peanut potatoes, lemons & fakir parsley root leaves . . . 145

moong dahl with early snowball cauliflower
    & bloomsdale long-standing spinach 149

charleston "ice cream" 152

charentais melon soup with homemade yogurt & mint 153

a fancy late spring lunch

salad of tender greens, crispy capers, pancetta & almonds 157

soft shell crab, broccoli rabe & chipotle sandwiches. 158

apricots poached with ginger & lime 161

summer *164*

in honor of bernard loiseau

eggplant caviar with zucchini sauce. 168

frog legs with garlic purée & parsley sauce. 172

blackberries with ricotta, granola & wild honey 175

luncheon, family style

radishes three ways. 179

smoked whitefish with onion purée & pea shoots. 180

purslane with baby beets, braised beet greens & bacon 182

roasted halibut with spinach & cucumber-saffron vinaigrette 184

strawberries in red wine with hibiscus tea ice cream 186

a midsummer's night picnic

grilled figs wrapped in pancetta 188

walker's pesto passion 190

orzo, radicchio, chick pea & herb salad 192

rhubarb tarts 195

saint euphrosynos

updated waldorf salad. 200

braised lamb shanks with apples, turnips & lentils. 202

classic tart tatin 204

INDEX   209

ACKNOWLEDGEMENTS   223

the cooks' house

local sustainable cuisine

Eric Patterson | Jennifer Blakeslee | Theresa Patterson
chef/owner | chef/owner |

T.231.946.8700   www.thecookshouse.typepad.com

introduction

JEN AND I MET when I was the chef at Andre's French Restaurant in Las Vegas, Nevada. She was my sous chef, and over the course of a few years we developed a great working friendship. Occasionally, we'd talk about doing something on our own. It was during one of these "what if" conversations that I mentioned to her that my wife, Theresa, and I had been investigating different parts of the country to move to and open a restaurant that focused on local products. Jen immediately suggested her childhood home of Traverse City, Michigan. Since I had never heard of Traverse City, I had to do some online research to see if it had what we were looking for in a location. Was it ever! Not long after, we gave our notices and moved up here — for Theresa and I, sight unseen. None of us had much money, but we did have a business plan and good ideas. We moved trusting that if we allowed things to happen naturally, it would all work out.

The Cooks' House restaurant has but 6 tables and 19 seats. It measures a total of 450 square feet including the kitchen, dishroom and restroom. Guests often comment that they can't believe we're able to produce such amazing food in such a small space — our kitchen being smaller than most home kitchens. But we think it's a testimony to the fact that extraordinary food comes not from fancy kitchens or large staffs but through hard work, passion, and above all else, great ingredients.

When it comes to top-notch ingredients, Michigan will give a run for the money to anywhere else on earth. We have small farmers who lovingly grow the highest quality produce. The cheese made in Michigan is one of our best kept secrets. There is grass fed beef, beautiful lamb, incredible pork and small-scale ranchers who are beginning to raise a variety of heritage livestock. We have old-timers who make superb sausages. The milk we get is never more than a couple days old and of the best quality. Depending of the time of year, we can get morels, golden chanterelles, porcinis, hen of the woods, hunter's hearts and other wild mushrooms foraged by Jim Moses, the area's foremost expert. There are wild leeks, wild watercress, wild roses, wild fennel — all of which we use when we can get them. Marco-Pierre White is fond of saying that Mother Nature is the true artist. We take his advice in this matter, choosing to let the ingredients speak for themselves while keeping our dishes as simple as possible. With all the world-class products we have to work with, keeping the dishes simple is only too easy.

JEN AND I SHARE a common philosophy of cooking although we approach food differently. My food tends to be more hoity-toity, while Jen's is more relaxed and whimsical. Truth be told, Jen is the more creative of us. She can spout ideas all day long while I struggle to articulate just one. Our individual approaches come

from our backgrounds. Jen has spent time in Italy and Mexico, cooking in small, hole-in-the-wall restaurants and learning from grandmothers the secrets of old cuisines. She has also worked as a private chef, where flexibility is essential, and as a restaurant chef, where she brought all her worldly experience together under one cap. On the other hand, I've spent most of my time in high-end French restaurants where the emphasis was on precision, perfection and technique. In this environment, creativity is kept in check and chefs are guarded when it comes to implementing new ideas. What has happened in The Cooks' House is that we've mutually influenced each other's style. Jen has helped me to tone it down a bit and not be afraid when an idea sounds odd; I've helped refine her food.

THIS COOKBOOK IS MORE than a collection of recipes. In fact, the recipes are the least important part. Our approach to cooking is where we'd like to shine the light. Our philosophy begins with the belief that cooking has very little to do with following a recipe word for word. We believe that a person only truly begins to *cook* when she or he brings their whole life into the act. In other words, we don't want you to recreate the recipes in this book; we want you to *use* them to find your own voice. Many of the recipes have, at times, instructions that may be a little vague or don't offer exact times or amounts — this is for a reason. We hope you'll feel your way around the food and learn to trust your own tastes. Listen to what the dish wants to do. Our primary goal is to inspire you to go out and cook something you can call your own.

In that spirit, we offer these elements for creative cooking:

1)   Start asking yourself the question when you're cooking, *What am I doing?* Are you just following orders or are you anticipating how the addition — or subtraction — of an ingredient or technique might affect the dish? Creation takes imagination.

2)   Always keep the aesthetics in mind. The dish must be pleasing to all your senses. Work on seeing the finished plate in your head before you even start. Can you taste it? How does it look on the plate? This takes lots of practice, but it's a skill well worth developing as it will save you loads of time and money.

3)   As you're imagining the taste and presentation of the dish, think in terms of contrast and balance. Each dish has to have contrast and balance, e.g., creamy / crunchy. The creativity comes from finding new ways to do this.

4)   Start storing up in your memory food combinations and use them as reference points when walking down the market aisles. For instance, I know tomatoes and rabbit go well together. I also know rabbit and chocolate go well together… I wonder how tomatoes and chocolate will work? Stretch your imagination to make associations. This also works well with techniques: Can you use a certain technique in a new way?

5)   This is a big one: Everything, and we mean *everything* in a dish has to have meaning and purpose. If you can't justify the presence of an ingredient or the purpose of a certain step or technique, then said ingredient has no place on the plate. Constantly question your every move: *Do I really need this? Will this be made better by … ?* Question, question, question.

6)   Break the rules, but only after you question, question, question.

7)   Buy cookbooks by recommended chefs and read them. We read cook books constantly, looking for ideas and approaches and we regularly find new techniques for old practices. Don't forget to read the introductions to these books. Read the chef's notes. Great cookbooks offer the simplest way to get a cooking education without spending years in professional kitchens. Let the chef/author be your teacher.

THAT LAST RULE reminds us to recognize those who help make our food as good as it is. For us at The Cooks' House, we'd like to thank our outstanding staff of cooks and servers and the farmers and producers who supply us with such amazing products.

Personally, there are two chefs who have had the most direct influence on my career. The first is Chef Dave Nelson of the Colonial Steak House in my home town of Oakley, Kansas. It was Dave who let me take my first steps in the kitchen when I was fourteen, and it was under him I learned the basics and the love of cooking.

The other is Chef Andre Rochat, who I consider my mentor. Andre taught me the fine art of cookery. He showed me the heights food can attain. I have said that I didn't know how to boil water until Andre taught me; he is the one I credit most with the success I have found as a chef.

Jennifer has a harder time pinning down any one person who had the most influence on her cooking, but she settled on those who graciously invited her into their kitchens when she was traveling around Italy, Mexico and the western slopes of Colorado. From these cooks, she says she learned that great food has soul, and that that soul doesn't come from an impressive cooking pedigree or from formal education but from a love and passion that can only come from within.

Now go out and cook something!

how to use this book

Unless otherwise noted, all the recipes are for four people.

There are certain items we expect any cook to have in their pantries, and because of this, when the amounts are small, we don't list them in the ingredients list. These include things like butter, olive oil, salt, pepper, sugar, flour, milk, certain spices, aluminum foil ... the basics. But as with everything we use in our kitchen, the quality of basic ingredients are as important as the quality of the main ingredients. With that in mind, always use good butter, extra virgin olive oil, sea or Kosher salt, whole pepper corns and spices ground when we need them, unprocessed sugar, unbleached flour, etc. And don't forget the chicken stock; there's a recipe on page 113.

Scattered throughout the book are thoughts, stories, words of caution, insights into a chef's life and so on, put there to show you how our cooking is more than just a collection of recipes. For us, cooking is life: it's our literature and our connection with the community, it's our history and our baby. And now, we'd like to say,

Our house is your house.

Make yourself at home.

33 moments of happiness

Chin Shengt'an was a seventeenth century scholar who, while stuck in a temple for ten days during foul weather, collaborated with a friend to write 33 happy moments. While I don't find all, or even most of Chin's moments particularly happy, I do re-read them from time to time as a way to consider my own happy moments at home, in the kitchen and, in a word, in life. Ah, is this not happiness?

1

autumn

The summer has been good to us,
and with the coming of winter
we need to bring in from the elements
those things that will sustain us
when the snows come.

mesón mexicano

warm cactus & chorizo salad

chicken thighs braised in chocolate, chili peppers, dried cherries & stewed tomatoes

mother-in-law's flour tortillas

caramel flan

harvest celebration

mussel, white bean, kale & garlic soup

ragout of root vegetables & mushrooms

whole roasted beef tenderloin with wilted arugula & crushed fingerling potatoes

blue cheese cheesecake with pear compote

a menu for the melancholy

artichoke soup with walnuts & parsley

salad of roasted beets, beet greens & tatsoi with freshly grated ginger and chives

trout poached in miso broth with baby bok choy & burdock root

stewed plums with vanilla and muscat

late autumn

turnip soup with turnip greens & bacon

roast pheasant with cauliflower salad & bread sauce

warm indian creamed rice with pomegranates & pistachios

mesón mexicano

warm cactus & chorizo salad

chicken thighs braised in chocolate, chili peppers,
dried cherries & stewed tomatoes

mother-in-law's flour tortillas

caramel flan

I'M SCOTTISH BY BIRTH but I tell people I'm half-Mexican
by marriage. You see, my wife is this beautiful Latina who has
accepted me into her colorful and richly beautiful culture.
I offer this menu as homage to my adopted heritage.   — E.P.

warm cactus & chorizo salad

5 cups white vinegar

4 tablespoons sugar

2 teaspoons whole coriander seed, toasted over high heat until you can smell it (Make sure to shake the seeds so they don't burn on one side.)

12 or so pearl onions, peeled

1 serrano pepper, left whole

zest of 2 limes, not grated but peeled off in large pieces with a vegetable peeler (Be careful to not get too much of the white pithy part.)

3 pear cactus pads, **thorns** removed, cut into $1/4$-inch strips and put into a bowl large enough to hold them comfortably

$1/2$ cup cabbage, cut into 3-inch slices about $1/4$-inch thick

3 tablespoons fresh, chopped cilantro

$1/3$ cup olive oil

1 or 2 chorizo sausages, depending on their size

$1/4$ cup pine nuts, toasted (You could also use toasted pumpkin seeds, or both seeds together.)

1 apple, something like Braeburn, Jonathan Gold, or Gala, crisp and sweet

> Holding the pear in a gloved hand and using a paring knife, slice the **thorns** off one by one. Be careful not to cut too deeply into the cactus flesh.

Put the vinegar and sugar in a pot and bring to a boil. Add the coriander seeds and onions. Let simmer for 4 minutes. After 4 minutes turn off the heat and add the serrano pepper, salt and the lime zest. Pour the mixture over the cactus until it just covers the cactus. Allow to cool, then add the cabbage, cilantro and olive oil to the mixture.

Remove the chorizo from their skins. Put a 10-inch frying pan with a little oil on medium heat. Add the chorizo once the oil is hot. Cook until done and drain on a paper towel.

to serve:

Cut the apple into julienne strips and toss with olive oil and a pinch of salt.

Arrange the cactus on a serving dish and sprinkle on the chorizo. Top with the pine nuts and apple.

The purpose of the **apple** is to add crunch and sweetness to counter the spicy bite of the chorizo. Remember to always think ying and yang in cooking. Balance creamy with crunch, sweet with spicy, fatty with acidic, and so on. There may be times when you'll want something to stand out—like tartness or spiciness—but even then you'll need something in the background pulling towards balance. Take this salad, for instance. One could always add raisins to counter the spicy chorizo, but there is still the softness of the salad to deal with. Perhaps, in this case, you could use jicama, or chayote squash, to add the crunch. Just because we decided to use apples doesn't mean you can't take a different route. Often the decision is simply what you feel like, what your style of cooking is, or what's available.

chicken thighs braised in chocolate, chili peppers, dried cherries & stewed tomatoes

3 dried ancho chilies
2 dried New Mexico chilies

8 chicken thighs
1 onion, diced small
1 teaspoon cumin seed
1 teaspoon coriander seed
1 teaspoon fennel seed
1/4 cup raisins
3 1/2 ounces Mexican chocolate broken up into small
    chunks (We have to insist on Mexican chocolate for this
    one. Mexican chocolate is made differently than other
    chocolate. It has cinnamon, coarse sugar and bits of cacao.
    The flavor is truly unique and very suited for this dish.)
1 cinnamon stick
2 bottles of Mexican beer (Any pilsner or lager will substitute.
    We use Bell's "Lager of the Lakes" since we like to stay as
    local as possible.)

5-7 medium-sized tomatoes, cut in half and the seeds
    squeezed out (It is very important that these tomatoes
    are ripe. In fact, if you have some that are getting a bit over-
    ripe, they would be great in this recipe.)
1 onion, one half sliced with the grain, the other diced
1/4 cup white wine
sprigs fresh cilantro

1/4 cup toasted pumpkin seeds

for the chili peppers:
De-stem and de-seed the chilies.

You will want to toast the chilies because this gives them a better flavor.

In a pan, heat 2 tablespoons of oil over medium. When the oil is hot, add a couple of chilies and press them lightly into the bottom of the pan

Since I'm no expert in **chilies**, I had to research the reason for toasting, and for this I turned to the cookbooks of Rick Bayless. Bayless is the chef/owner of Frontera Grill and Topolobampo in Chicago, and one of the foremost experts in the world on traditional Mexican cuisine. As many of my friends and family will contest, I am a bona-fide chef groupie, and Bayless is one of the chefs I look to as a role model.

Chef Bayless says that toasting chilies will make the sauce more complex by adding a hint of char and smokiness to balance the chili's natural astringency. There are two ways to roast a chili, according to the *maestro*. There's oil-toasting and there's dry-toasting. Oil-toasting is used for dishes like ours, as it yields a more thorough and velvety result. Dry-toasting produces a less mellow taste. —E.P.

with a spatula. When you begin to smell them, turn them over and toast the other side. Repeat until all the chilies are toasted. Be careful that the parts of the chilies touching the oil remain a nice brown color. We are the first to proclaim that black is beautiful, but in this case, not so much. Keep the chilies handy until needed. Reserve the cooking oil.

for the rest of the dish:

In a pot just large enough to hold the chicken and other ingredients, heat the leftover chili oil over medium-high. When it begins to smoke a little, add 4 of the chicken thighs, browning them on both sides. Set aside on a plate and repeat with the others.

Turn the heat down to medium and add the diced onion, cumin seeds, coriander seeds and fennel seeds. Sauté for about 2 minutes, or until you begin to smell the spices and the onions are soft with a slight browning.

Add the chicken back in, plus the chilies, raisins, chocolate, cinnamon stick and beer. If you need to add more liquid, use chicken stock or water, but it isn't necessary that the chicken be entirely covered.

Now, there are a couple of options. You can put the pot in a 325-degree oven, or you can simmer it on the stovetop. Regardless, you should first bring the stew to a boil and skim off any foamy gunk that comes to the top. Cover and cook for about 45-60 minutes. Check the doneness of the chicken by pricking it and looking at the color of the juice (it should be clear) or by using a meat thermometer (it should read 140 degrees).

for the tomatoes:

While the chicken is cooking, prepare the tomatoes. Place 2 tablespoons of olive oil in a 3-quart pot and heat on medium. Add the onion slices and let cook until translucent and soft. Stir in the tomatoes and wine, season with salt and a little pepper. Cover and cook on medium-low for 20 minutes. Uncover and add the cilantro. Adjust the seasoning. Keep hot.

to finish:

When the chicken is done, remove the thighs from the stew and keep warm.

Strain the cooking juice into a 3-quart saucepan and add the juice from the stewed tomatoes. Reduce the liquid over medium-high heat until it measures about 4-5 cups. In 2 batches, purée the pumpkin seeds into the cooking liquid. Make sure the purée is very smooth. Adjust the seasoning.

to serve:

Put a pile of tomatoes into the middle of a bowl and rest 2 thighs against it. Spoon some of the sauce over the top. There should be a decent amount of sauce in the bowl, but not so much as to make it look like soup. Garnish with a couple sprigs of cilantro and a sprinkling of pumpkin seeds.

OF BULLS AND BALLERINAS

THERE ARE TWO TYPES of cooks in the world: the bull and the ballerina. Each has their place and individual role in the kitchen, and every kitchen needs a healthy mixture of the two. The exact mix, however, is entirely dependent on the individual kitchen. For instance, if the kitchen is pumping out buffets or banquets for hundreds, or even thousands of people, on a regular basis, then it will need more raging bulls. If it's a high-end restaurant producing world class cuisine for which the average guest bill is above $100.00 per person, then it will need a fair number of dainty ballerinas. Get the picture? Here's something else: Bulls cannot be ballerinas and ballerinas cannot be bulls. Believe me, I've tried to convert each type. But I am convinced that each can learn from the other. And every cook should strive to achieve a happy medium between the two.

Let me give you examples of each extreme. Once, I had this kid working for me who was a mess on the line. No matter how hard he tried, he could not get the food on the plate the way I wanted it. Tell him you wanted a *dollop* and he would *plop*. He had absolutely no grace in his movements, which showed on his plates, but when I moved him to prep he really came into his own. This kid was amazing when it came to defeating prep lists. We would leave him lists of epic proportions and I'd be damned if he wouldn't have them completed every time we came in for the shift. It got to the point where we'd add any old thing we could think of just to see if he could get it done. He did, each and every time. His speed was truly amazing. He not only completed his lists, he did so without screwing anything up.

Now, let's contrast him with a little ballerina who worked for me. I'll call her Jane. Jane was painfully slow at everything, but what she did, she did well. She worked for me as an intern for a couple of months during our off-season. We would do 20 people and it would feel like we did 100.

It took Jane forever to plate anything. I don't know how many times I'd find myself pounding the table, screaming that I needed HER dish to SELL the order. Oh, oh, oh, she would buzz around the kitchen busy as a bee. She was always doing something at 100 mph but getting nothing done. She'd come in two hours early to start her prep and still not be ready when we opened. Sure, she could make beautiful food, but my God, continents move quicker than she did.

What you want to aim for in your work is that happy balance between the two examples above. The two most important characteristics in a line cook are speed and precision. Speed is the bull. Precision is the ballerina. A well-balanced cook, no matter on which side of the line he or she may fall, will have characteristics of both, though one will always outshine the other. Discover which one you are and play to your strengths.

What am I? I'm a ballerina, which is good, because I look *fabulous* in a tutu.

—E.P.

mother-in-law's tortillas

María taught me to make these just like her mother taught her — by eye and feel. Actually, to write this recipe down, I had to go upstairs and make a batch so I could get measurements.   —E.P.

3 1/4 cups unbleached flour
2 teaspoons baking powder
1 teaspoon salt
3 ounces lard
1/2 ounce bacon fat
1 1/4 cups warm water

Put the flour, baking powder and salt into a bowl and mix well. Cut the lard and bacon fat into the flour until the mixture resembles coarse corn meal. Make a well in the middle of the mixture, and pour some of the water into the well. Mix the water and flour together a little at a time until a dough is formed. Knead the dough for a couple of minutes, cover and let rest for one hour.

Once the dough has rested, divide into 8 balls.

There are a couple of ways to roll out the tortillas. You can use a rolling pin, or you can try our favorite "traditional" method, which is stretching the tortillas. Place a dough ball on a floured surface and gently press out from the center until you get a flattish disc 6-8-inches in diameter. Pick up the disc and start stretching it while rotating in one direction. This takes some practice, but in the end it makes a nicer tortilla.

Cook the tortillas as soon as you finish rolling or stretching them. Heat a flat, sideless, cast iron pan to high heat. Place an uncooked tortilla on the hot pan. This may create some smoke so have your hood fan on. Cook on the first side for about 30-45 seconds or until nicely browned. Flip and cook for another 30 seconds or so.

Cook the tortillas as quickly as possible. If the heat's not high enough, the tortillas will stay too long on the fire and become crackers.

María uses her fingers to flip tortillas and, from what we gather, so does every other true tortilla maker. Being gringos, we like to use a spatula. Once the tortilla is cooked, let it cool before stacking. If you stack warm tortillas, they'll stick together as they cool.

caramel flan

We hemmed and hawed over including this recipe as flan is made pretty much the same way by most pastry chefs around the world. But, for the most part, chefs are not content with the plain and straightforward. Our inner chef was screaming to make this flan different — to add some chilies, or a spice of some sort, but we held back for two reasons. First, the basic flan recipe gives you the blank canvas to write on and add to as your own inner chef demands. Second, this recipe honestly represents the flan most often enjoyed in Mexican cookbooks and restaurants.

$\frac{1}{2}$ cup sugar
$\frac{1}{2}$ cup water
2 cups milk
$\frac{1}{3}$ cup sugar
2 whole eggs
2 egg yolks
1 vanilla bean, split in half
Either a one-quart ovenproof mold or four
      1-cup ovenproof ramekins

If your stove is like ours, you'll notice the sugar **browns** unevenly. When this happens, simply pick up the pan and rotate it while tilting. Do not, we repeat, **do not** shake the pan, as this will cause the sugar to crystallize, at which point you can throw the whole thing away and start over.

To clean the pan, fill it with some water and bring to a boil. The sugar (or most any other crusty mess) will dissolve and you can pour it out.

for the caramel:

Put the sugar and water in a pan and turn the heat on high. Once the water boils, give it a good stir to dissolve the sugar. Let the sugar-water boil until it begins to brown.

As the sugar begins to brown, keep a close eye on it as it can go from golden to burnt at the speed of light. What you want is a deep brown color. When you've got that, pour the sugar into the molds or ramekins. Now, quickly spin the mold or ramekins to spread the caramel evenly on the bottom. If the sugar cools before you can spread it, heat the dish in a microwave for a few seconds and try again.

to make the flan:

Preheat oven to 350 degrees.

Put the milk into a pot large enough to hold it. Scrape the vanilla bean seeds into the milk and then add the pod. Bring to a boil.

Once the mixture boils, turn off the heat and add the sugar, stirring until it dissolves. Let stand for 10 minutes.

Mix the whole eggs and the egg yolks together in a bowl. Add $\frac{1}{4}$ cup of the hot milk to the eggs and mix well. Now, slowly add the rest of the milk, discarding the vanilla bean pod.

Ladle this mixture into the mold.

Place the mold in a pan large enough to hold it. Fill the pan with water until it reaches halfway up the sides of the mold. Bake the flan in the oven for 30 minutes. Check for doneness by inserting a knife: if it comes out clean, it's done. Cool the flan in the refrigerator.

to serve:
Run a knife around the edge of the cooled mold to loosen the flan. Cover the mold with a serving dish and invert in one swift motion, gently shaking until you feel the flan release. Flan is very good served with whipped cream.

A couple comes into the restaurant for their anniversary but it is soon apparent they don't have much money to spend. The man, though he doesn't readily show it, wishes he had more so his beautiful bride could have a truly sumptuous dinner. Without making a show of it, we roll out the red carpet, sending them extra courses on top of what they have already ordered. They leave satiated and happy without ever knowing what we did. Ah, is this not happiness?

a note on making caramel:

MAKING CARAMEL is both easy and difficult. The first thing to remember is that hot, melted sugar is HOT! When working with caramelized sugar be **extremely** careful not to burn yourself. (Of course, when you do finally spill some on yourself, you can check off another requirement for becoming a true chef.) Hot caramelized sugar sticks to the skin like nothing else and there is no getting it off easily. The good news is that eventually the sugar will cool down enough for you to pick it off; the bad news is that once you get the sugar off, you'll be left with a blister.

harvest celebration

mussel, white bean, kale & garlic soup

ragout of root vegetables and mushrooms

whole roasted beef tenderloin
with wilted arugula and crushed fingerling potatoes

blue cheese cheesecake with pear compote

AUTUMN IS A BUSY TIME FOR FARMERS, but it's the busiest time for winemakers. The grapes are perfectly ripe and need picking fast, and winemakers spend many a sleepless night getting the fruit off the vines and into the vats.

When creating a menu, it's important to keep the occasion foremost in mind. Here, we wanted to celebrate both the harvest of food and the harvest of drink. There are times, though, when you may have some special bottles of wine you want show off for themselves. Then, the food should take a back seat to the wine and feature flavors that don't compete. At other times you may have a star ingredient, fresh porcinis, for example. Then, you'll want the wine to stay in the background, keeping the attention on the mushrooms.

In this menu, however, the food and the wine are equal partners, and wine pairing suggestions have been offered for each course.

mussel, white bean, kale & garlic soup

Serve with Chenin Blanc or Dry Riesling

1/2 carrot, cut in small dice
1 large onion, cut in small dice
1/2 stalk celery, cut in small dice
4 heads whole garlic, peeled and
    sliced in half lengthwise
sprig of thyme
2 tablespoons olive oil
2 cups white wine (If possible, use the same wine you'll
    be drinking with the soup. It makes the wine/food
    pairing more consistent.)
3/4 gallon water
5 or 6 black peppercorns

1 1/2 pounds fresh mussels

2 cups cooked white beans
2 bunches kale, stalks removed and discarded,
    leaves chopped

While there are over 400 varieties of **garlic**, they all fall into two basic categories: hardneck and softneck. The softneck types are what you most commonly find in supermarkets for they tend to store better. Hardneck garlics are stronger and more assertive — trying the two side by side will reveal softnecks as bland and boring.

Make a court-bullion by putting the carrots, celery, onions, garlic and the sprig of thyme into a 5-quart pot with about 2 tablespoons olive oil. Cover and cook over low heat until the onions are translucent and the vegetables soft. Stir frequently as you don't want the vegetables or garlic to color.

Add the wine, water and peppercorns and bring to a boil. Once boiling, reduce heat to a simmer and cook uncovered for 25 minutes.

While the bullion is cooking, clean the mussels. Wash them and remove any beards — these are the coarse threads and they need to be pulled off. Discard the mussels that have died.

The trick to knowing if **mollusks** are still alive is to insert a knife gently into the open shell, touching the meat. If there is no reaction, then the creature is dead.

When the bullion has cooked for 25 minutes, turn the heat to high and get a good boil going. Plunge those mussels into the stock. Cover and let cook until they pop open — this may take no more than 1 1/2 minutes. Remove them from the stock and allow to cool. When you can handle them, separate the meat from the shells. Discard the shells and any unopened mussels.

To the stock, add the chopped kale and cooked white beans. Bring to a boil once again and cook until the kale is tender, about 5 minutes. Put the mussels back in the stock and stir, simmering for about 1 more minute. Season with salt and ladle into bowls.

This soup is very good when served with crusty bread.

VINTAGE POETRY

IT SAYS in the Bible that *drink maketh the heart of man merry* — and
who are we to argue with such an august book? So to keep us merry,
here are some poems ...

O, for a draught of vintage! that hath been
Cool'd a long age in the deep-delv'd earth,
Tasting of Flora and the country-green,
Dance, and Provencal song, and sunburnt mirth!
Oh, for a beaker of the warm South,
Full of the true, the blushful Hippocrene,
With beaded bubbles winking at the brim,
And purple-stained mouth;
That I might drink and leave the world unseen,
And with thee fade away into the forest dim.

—JOHN KEATS

Not drunk is he who from the floor
Can rise alone and still drink more;
But drunk is he who prostrate lies
Without the power to move or rise.

—THOMAS LOVE PEACOCK

But if at the Church they would give us some ale,
And a pleasant fire our souls to regale,
We'd sing and we'd pray all the live-long day,
And never once wish from the Church to stray.

—ANON

3 Out of the blue, a dear friend, whom I've not spoken
with for many years, contacts me for advice on a recipe,
and because of this we rekindle our friendship. Ah, is
this not happiness?

ragout of root vegetables & mushrooms

Serve with Chardonnay, Dry Rose or Sauvignon Blanc

1/3 pound Parmesan cheese rind (This is optional, but if you buy your Parmesano Reggiano fresh we suggest you save the rinds to make a broth. The Parmesan will take this ragout to a different level.)

2 peeled garlic cloves

4 cups chicken stock

2 cups mixed root vegetables (Pick what's available and nice. Baby root vegetables are great for this recipe.)

1 medium shallot, finely chopped

2 cups wild mushrooms (Again, this depends on what's available. Substitute if you can't find wild mushrooms.)

2 sprigs of thyme

1 tablespoon chopped mixed herbs

4 pieces of bread cut into 3-inch rounds

Chicken stock is one of those items no kitchen should ever be without. It's best to make your own (see page 113 for these simple instructions), but there are some very good boxed ones available. If you do buy boxed, look for the lowest sodium possible. No sodium is ideal.

Heat oven to 350 degrees.

Place the Parmesan rind, garlic cloves and chicken stock in a 2-quart pot and bring to a boil. Turn down to a simmer and allow to cook for 30 minutes. Strain broth into a 1-quart pan and bring to a rapid simmer. Simmer until reduced to 1 cup.

Wash your vegetables. If you're using baby vegetables, the only thing you might need to do is trim the tops and remove any roots.

Take a 12- by 12-inch square of foil and put it into a frying pan. (Make sure the pan is non-Teflon and the handle is oven-safe.) Place the vegetables (not the mushrooms) on the foil and top with a couple sprigs of thyme. Sprinkle well with olive oil, salt and pepper. Fold the foil to form a package. Roast for 30 minutes.

When your vegetables are cooked, place them on a plate and discard the foil. Using the same pan, now on the stovetop (be careful of that hot handle), cook the shallots over medium-low until soft and translucent. Add the mushrooms, season with salt and pepper and cook for 1 1/2 minutes. Stir in the vegetables, Parmesan broth and a hazelnut-sized piece of butter. Bring to a boil and cook until the broth is reduced and a nice sauce — one that coats the back of a spoon — has formed. Add herbs, mix and adjust the seasoning.

Now, fill a 10-inch frying pan with 1/4-inch of olive oil and turn to medium-high heat. When oil is hot, fry 1 piece of bread at a time until golden brown on both sides. Drain on a towel.

Be careful about reducing too much, as it will cause the sauce to break and become greasy. Of course, not cooking it enough will leave a watery sauce. You're looking for a sauce that clings to the vegetables and mushrooms. See page 179 about what to do if a sauce breaks.

to plate:

Place a crouton in the middle of each plate. Spoon some ragout over the top of the crouton and garnish with a sprig of an herb.

whole roasted beef tenderloin with wilted arugula & crushed fingerling potatoes

Serve with Zinfandel, Pinot Noir or Shiraz

2 pounds whole filet tenderloin (Ask your butcher to give you the center of the tenderloin. Don't have it cut into steaks.)
Kosher salt
butter

1 1/2 medium shallot, minced
4 cups red wine (Preferably the same wine you will be drinking with the dish.)
2 cups chicken stock
2 teaspoons sugar
2 black peppercorns
sprig of thyme

4 fingerling potatoes, a little on the larger side

4 handfuls arugula
Kosher salt

for the filet:

Preheat oven to 425 degrees.

Season the filet on all sides with Kosher salt and pepper. Place in a pan on a roasting rack. Smear the top of the filet with a good amount of soft butter. Place in the oven and roast for 25 minutes, basting every 5 minutes with the melted butter from the bottom of the pan. This keeps the filet from drying out and also adds savoryness. After the filet has cooked for 25 minutes, check the temperature using a thermometer. It should read no more than 122 degrees. Remove it from the oven and allow it to rest for 15 minutes.

We differ from most guides when it comes to cooked meat temperatures. We think the guides are about 5 degrees off. Rare should be 115 degrees, medium-rare around 122, medium is no more than 130 and medium-well is 135 and above. Five degrees might not sound like much of a difference, but in the finished product it's a lot, for during the 15-minute resting period the meat continues and finishes cooking.

What happens during the oven cooking is that the juices rush to the center of the meat and the tissues tighten. If the meat is removed from the oven and not allowed to rest, the juices drain out immediately, right onto the plate. By resting the meat you're allowing the tissues to relax and the juices to redistribute themselves, finishing the cooking process.

for the sauce:

While the filet is roasting, sweat the chopped shallot in a little butter over medium heat.

When the shallot is soft, add the wine, chicken stock, sugar, peppercorns and thyme sprig. Turn up the heat and bring to a rapid simmer. Allow to cook until the sauce has reduced to a little under 1 cup. Take it off the heat and whisk in a piece of butter the size of a hazelnut. Season with salt and strain into a gravy cup. Keep warm.

for the potatoes:

While the filet is cooking, place potatoes in a pan and fill with enough water to cover. Add 2 tablespoons salt.

Boil the potatoes until you can insert a knife without resistance. Remove them from the water and keep warm under an over-turned bowl.

to finish & plate:

Just before you're ready to serve the dish, toss the arugula with the sliced shallot, a bit of olive oil and a pinch of salt in a pan over low heat. Stir until the arugula's just warm and ever-so-slightly wilted.

Cut the potatoes in half and place them in the middle of the upper half of each plate. Crush the potatoes with a fork and drizzle with olive oil. Add a pinch of kosher salt. Spread the arugula mixture over the potatoes.

Slice the filet into 12 pieces. Arrange 3 slices per plate in a half moon around the arugula and potatoes on the bottom half of the plates. Pour some sauce on top of the filet slices.

Sweating means to cook on low temperature without browning. The idea behind the technique is to bring out the sweetness while getting rid of any bitterness in the vegetable.

Salting the water adequately when you boil potatoes, pasta, rice, grains, vegetables, etc., is extremely important as you won't be able to replace it at the end. Salting the water makes for a more even, rounded saltiness; salting at the end makes the taste sharper and more pronounced.

The amount of salt will vary according to what you're cooking. Anything with a thick skin, for example, needs a liberal amount of salt in order to penetrate to the flesh inside.

Potatoes left in their **cooking water** will take on a reheated taste.

I hire a dishwasher who has had some bad breaks in life. He has little education and a record. After a few months of washing dishes he shows an interest in learning to cook and I teach him. He moves on and a few years go by. One day I hear from him and learn that cooking has given him a good life. Ah, is this not happiness?

5 The restaurant is full and the kitchen is very busy but the cooks are all dancing with each other flawlessly. The sound of pots hitting the stovetop. The sound of knives on the cutting boards. The sound of the chef calling her tickets. Ah, is this not happiness?

blue cheese cheesecake
with pear compote

Serve with Champagne, Sparkling Wine, Ice Wine or Sauternes

1 cup sugar
3 tablespoons flour
5 eggs
2 pounds cream cheese, room temperature
8 ounces blue cheese, broken into small pieces
  (We like creamier blues for this.)

6 firm, ripe pears
2 cups Riesling wine
$1/2$ cup sugar
1 vanilla bean, cut in half lengthwise
zest of $1/2$ orange
juice of $1/2$ lemon

for the cake:
Preheat oven to 350 degrees.

Grease a 9-inch springform pan.

Put 1 cup sugar, flour, eggs and cream cheese in a bowl. Using an electric mixer, mix until smooth. Carefully fold in the blue cheese. Be careful not to over-mix or you'll end up with a grey cake. Pour into the springform pan. Bake for 45 minutes or until a toothpick inserted comes out clean. Refrigerate for at least 6 hours before unmolding.

for the pear compote:
Cut the pears into $1/2$-inch cubes — we prefer not to peel them. Combine the wine and $1/2$ cup sugar in a 4-quart pot. Bring to a boil, stirring to dissolve the sugar. Add vanilla bean, pears and orange zest. Cook for 5 minutes — the pears will get tender and the sauce will thicken — then pour into a bowl. Add the lemon juice, mix well and cool.

to plate:
Cut the cheesecake into slices. In the center of a plate, place a slice of cheesecake, and next to it, a good-sized scoop of the compote.

HOW A COOK DEFINES HERSELF becomes a fundamental part of that individual's cuisine. For example, does the cook see herself as traditionalist? An artist? A mom just trying to get something healthy into the kids' bellies? When the cook picks up his pan does he handle it like a well-oiled machine? You see, if I were to give a basket of identical ingredients to the artist, the traditionalist, the mom, the craftsman, that basket would live a different life under the influence of each individual's philosophy.

I used to try to see myself as an artist, but in the back of my mind I was uncomfortable with the idea. Certainly, there are chefs who create edible works so delicate, so perfectly constructed, so beautiful in every aspect that they could be called art. These chefs create dishes that spur conversation about the nature of food and life itself. Art is often ineffable and artists themselves cerebral. They make food controversial and questionable and they ask for definitions. That is what artists do. That is not what I do.

I would place my food in the realm of craft, and by craft I mean works made with skill using knowledge that comes from tradition but applied to the present moment. A crafted item is often intended for practical purposes and with functionality in mind. Craft may not be something made perfectly, with exacting standards, but it is something that is skillfully made. In fact, I like to think that the flaws in a well-crafted item are the source of its unique and individual beauty. A crafted item, made with skill, has character, and its flaws are not from inattentiveness, but from life.

—E.P.

My son and I stop in at a store to buy something. While walking down one of the aisles we are stopped by someone who recognizes me because of the restaurant, and because of this my son feels proud. Ah, is this not happiness?

a menu for the melancholy

artichoke soup with walnuts & parsley

salad of roasted beets, beet greens & tatsoi
with freshly grated ginger and chives

trout poached in miso broth
with baby bok choy & burdock root

stewed plums with vanilla & muscat

AUTUMN IS MY TIME of melancholy. I know for a fact that
winter is coming, again, and I tend to look backward to the
long, warm days of summer. It's a struggle, but I believe that
autumn should really be a time to look forward. It is a time to
reap our rewards and to celebrate that inevitable change that
must come to all of us. By looking backward in longing, we miss
the harvest. And we also miss the thankfulness. —E.P.

artichoke soup with walnuts & parsley

3 lemons
6 **artichokes**, trimmed down
    to the bottoms

$1\frac{1}{2}$ cups butter
$1\frac{1}{2}$ cups flour
$\frac{1}{2}$ cup heavy cream
$\frac{1}{2}$ shallot, thinly sliced
$\frac{1}{4}$ cup chopped walnuts
1 teaspoon sugar
parsley, chopped

1. If the artichoke has thorns, snip them off.

2. Peel off the little leaves on the bottom. With a sharp knife, cut off the top, leaving $1\frac{1}{2}$ inches.

3. Hold the artichoke top-side up in your hand and using a utility knife, start removing the leaves by cutting around the diameter, being careful that you don't cut into the artichoke bottom.

4. Continue to cut until the only leaves left are those on top of the bottom.

5. Trim off the little patches of green you may have left behind and try to round out the bottom into a dome.

6. Now cut the leaves and heart from the top of the bottom; don't cut the bottom.

7. Put the artichoke bottom in a pan of water and lemon juice.

There is a tendency for cooks to add the **lemons** to the water after their juice has been squeezed out. This is a bad idea because the lemon rind contains oils that will make the water bitter, hence also making whatever is cooked in the water bitter.

Bring 8 cups of water to a boil in a 4-quart pot. Squeeze the juice of the **lemons** into the water.

Stir in a tablespoon of salt and add the artichoke bottoms to the water. Let them cook at medium boil until very tender — a knife should be inserted with no resistance at all.

After the bottoms are well cooked take them out of the water and set them on a plate on their sides to drain. Pour the cooking liquid into a container to keep for a few moments while you make the roux to thicken the soup — a water pitcher would be best, as you'll see in a bit.

In the same pot in which you cooked the artichokes, melt the butter. Using a whisk, stir the flour into the butter. Cook on medium heat for 1 minute, stirring constantly. Now, slowly pour in the hot reserved liquid. (If the liquid is in a pitcher, you can pour and whisk at the same time.) Once all the liquid has been added, set the stock to simmer for 25 minutes or so.

While the stock is simmering, remove the hearts from the artichoke bottoms and discard. Chop the bottoms into small pieces.
When the stock is ready, purée the artichoke bottoms in batches with the stock. Use a blender for this. Be aware that it's not necessary to use all of the stock. What you want is a soup that clings to the spoon. Whisk in the cream and $\frac{1}{4}$ cup butter. Adjust the seasoning.

Now, melt a walnut-sized piece of butter in a small fry pan over medium-low. Add the shallot and cook until soft and translucent. Turn up heat to medium-high and add the walnuts and 1 teaspoon sugar. Sauté, stirring all the while, until the walnuts are golden-brown. Add the chopped parsley. Drain on paper towel and lightly season with salt.

to plate:
Ladle the soup into 4 bowls and spoon equal portions of the walnut mixture in the center of each.

salad of roasted beets, beet greens & tatsoi with freshly grated ginger & chives

sprig of fresh thyme
1 large or 2 medium beets with greens
    removed (reserve the greens)
olive oil
1 medium shallot, finely chopped
$\frac{1}{4}$ cup chicken stock
4 handfuls tatsoi (If tatsoi is unavailable you
    can use spinach.)
verjus (If verjus is not available use rice vinegar.)
fresh ginger
fresh chives

Preheat oven to 350 degrees.

Put a 12- by 12-inch square of foil into a small ovenproof fry pan. Arrange the beets on the foil with the sprig of thyme, a sprinkle of salt and drizzle of olive oil. Fold in the sides to make a sealed package. Roast in the oven for 45 minutes or until a knife is easily inserted. Remove from the oven and allow to cool.

When the beets are cool enough to handle, peel and slice them into $\frac{1}{8}$-inch rounds. Toss them with a tablespoon or so of olive oil, add salt and set aside.

Heat a tablespoon of olive oil in a fry pan over medium and add the shallot. Sauté until soft and translucent. Add the beet greens and toss. Add the chicken stock. Turn up the heat to high and cook until the stock is almost completely reduced. Be sure to stir often so that the greens don't burn to the bottom.

While the greens are cooking, toss the tatsoi in olive oil and a bit of the verjus. The trick here is to add just enough oil to moisten the leaves and not so much verjus that it overpowers the olive oil. While tossing the salad add a pinch of salt.

A pinch of **salt** when making a salad is one of those little steps that make all the difference.

to plate:

Place the tatsoi in nice, neat piles on 4 plates. Arrange the beets over the tatsoi and place the warm greens on top of that. Fresh grated ginger and a sprinkle of chives complete each dish.

trout poached in miso broth with baby bok choy & burdock root

¹/₂ ounce giant kelp
¹/₂ ounce dried bonito flakes

8 baby bok choy

rice vinegar
1 burdock root
olive oil
soy sauce
sesame oil
red pepper flakes

4 lake trout fillets (Salmon can also be used.)
4 tablespoons white or yellow miso

The kelp, bonito flakes, and miso can be found in any Asian market.

for the dashi, a stock that's used extensively in Japanese cuisine:

Fill a 5-quart pot with 2 quarts water, add the giant kelp and slowly bring to a simmer. This should take about 15 minutes. When the water simmers, pierce the kelp with a knife. It should be tender. If not, turn the heat down and allow it to cook a little longer. Remove the kelp from the pot when it's done and discard.

Add the bonito flakes and turn the heat up to medium-high. Right before the water boils, turn the heat off completely. Allow the dashi to rest until the flakes have settled to the bottom. Strain out the flakes and discard.

for the bok choy:

Place the bok choy in a fry pan just large enough to hold them. Cover with the dashi (you will not use it all) and bring to a simmer. Continue simmering until a knife can be inserted without much resistance. Remove the bok choy from the dashi and keep warm.

for the burdock salad:

Place 1 tablespoon of rice vinegar and 4 cups of water in a bowl.

Peel the burdock root and cut into 1 ¹/₂-inch pieces. Immerse in the water solution.

Now, remove a single piece and cut into matchstick-sized slices, immediately replacing the pieces in the bowl as you finish. Burdock turns brown very easily, so it is important to keep it in the solution until it's ready to be cooked. When you've finished all the slicing, scoop the burdock out of the water and dry it on a towel.

Heat a sauté pan with 2 teaspoons of olive oil over high heat. As soon as the oil begins to smoke, add the burdock root. Toss the root in the oil a couple times, then allow it to cook for about 3 minutes or until it's soft but not mushy. Add 1 teaspoon of soy sauce, a few drops sesame oil and a pinch of red pepper flakes. Drain on a paper towel. Keep warm.

for the trout:
Season the trout with salt. In a pan just large enough to hold the fish, bring 3 cups of the dashi to a simmer and mix in 3 teaspoons of miso. Add the trout and poach for 5 minutes.

to plate:
Put 2 bok choy in each of 4 large bowls. Place the trout on top of the bok choy and the burdock root salad on top of that. Pour ⅓ cup of the miso broth over the trout and serve.

The look of a perfectly cooked piece of fish.
Ah, is this not happiness?

THE **TAOIST TALE** OF THE TAMING OF THE HARP

I ALWAYS KEEP A COPY of this tale in my kitchens. In fact, the same copy has been with me for years and it's getting a bit frail. It's from *The Book of Tea*, written by Okakura Kakuzo. To me, the story amounts to a cooking paradigm; if we cooks approached cooking the way Peiwoh does the harp, we'd make the most beautiful music.

Once in the hoary ages in the Ravine of Lungmen stood a Kiri tree, a veritable king of the forest. It reared its head to talk to the stars; its roots struck deep into the earth, mingling their bronzed coils with those of the silver dragon that slept beneath. And it came to pass that a mighty wizard made of this tree a wondrous harp, whose stubborn spirit should be tamed but by the greatest of musicians. For long the instrument was treasured by the Emperor of China, but all in vain were the efforts of those who in turn tried to draw melody from its strings. In response to their utmost strivings there came from the harp but harsh notes of disdain, ill-according with the songs they fain would sing. The harp refused to recognize a master.

At last came Peiwoh, the prince of harpists. With tender hand he caressed the harp as one might seek to soothe an unruly horse, and softly touched the chords. He sang of nature and the seasons, of high mountains and flowing waters, and all the memories of the tree awoke! Once more the sweet breath of spring played amidst its branches. The young cataracts, as they danced down the ravine, laughed to the budding flowers. Anon were heard the dreamy voices of summer with its myriad insects, the gentle pattering of rain, the wail of the cuckoo. Hark! a tiger roars, — the valley answers again. It is autumn; in the desert night, sharp like a sword gleams the moon upon the frosted grass. Now winter reigns, and through the snow-filled air swirl flocks of swans and rattling hailstones beat upon the boughs with fierce delight.

Then Peiwoh changed the key and sang of love. The forest swayed like an ardent swain deep lost in thought. On high, like a haughty maiden, swept a cloud bright and fair; but passing, trailed long shadows on the ground, black like despair. Again the mode was changed; Peiwoh sang of war, of clashing steel and trampling steeds. And in the harp arose the tempest of Lungmen, the dragon rode the lightning, the thundering avalanche crashed through the hills. In ecstasy the Celestial monarch asked Peiwoh wherein lay the secret of his victory. 'Sire,' he replied, 'others have failed because they sang but of themselves. I left the harp to choose its theme, and knew not truly whether the harp had been Peiwoh or Peiwoh were the harp.'

—E.P.

stewed plums
with vanilla & muscat

2 cups Muscat
$1/2$ cup + 2 teaspoons sugar
1 vanilla bean, cut in half
cinnamon stick
8 plums, halved and pits removed
(Make sure plums are not too ripe.)
1 cup heavy whipping cream

Bring the wine and $1/2$ cup sugar to a boil in a 4-quart pot. Stir until sugar is dissolved. Stir in the vanilla bean and cinnamon and let simmer on medium heat for 3 to 4 minutes. Add the plums, cooking until tender, about 7 to 10 minutes. Remove the plums with a slotted spoon and keep warm.

Reduce the syrup until slightly thickened, then remove from heat and allow to cool.

In a separate bowl, whip the cream and 2 teaspoons sugar until stiff.

To plate:
Divide the plums equally into 4 bowls. Pour on some of the cooled syrup and add a spoonful of whipped cream on top.

I've had a hard day and notice there are some dishes to be done. Going back to the dish room I lose myself in the water and soap and the weight of the plates, forgetting about everything else. Ah, is this not happiness?

THE LIST OF FIVE

I KEEP A LIST of the five worst dishes I've ever created for those times when I get a little too uppity about how good I think I am. These failures are all from early in my career, but they were so clearly awful that their bitterness lingers to this day. Here they are, in no particular order:

1) **Asparagus Consommé.** This looked very much like dirty dishwater and tasted almost as bad.

2) **Foie Gras Crepe Soufflé.** Think of a greasy, very thin pancake with some egg stuff in the middle of it. Nice.

3) **Grilled Pear Cactus with Black Bean Sauce.** Just when Southwestern cuisine could not get any worse, I popped this flavorless wonder on an unsuspecting public.

4) **Cream of Barley Soup.** Yes, I now know barley has a ton of starch in it and it's a very bad idea to hit it with an immersion blender. The best way to understand this one is to open a pail of wallpaper paste and dig in.

5) **Cherry Clafouti.** A truly magnificent dish when properly made. I misread the recipe and doubled the amount of flour. Needless to say, it had an impressive bounce. I have successfully made it a number of times since, but the first attempt was bad enough to warrant this dish a place on the list.

Looking at this list, two thoughts come to mind. First, success as a chef comes from throwing away a lot of mistakes. And second, it's not the ingredients' fault that a dish turns out badly, but the choices the chef makes in preparing those ingredients.

—E.P.

late autumn

turnip soup with turnip greens & bacon

roast pheasant with cauliflower salad & bread sauce

warm indian creamed rice
with pomegranates & pistachios

AUTUMN IS THE SEASON that teaches us the hard lesson of impermanence. It gives us the first sign that we don't live forever. And while this is a hard truth to learn, autumn also shows us the impermanence of death.

In his book, *No Death, No Fear*, Thich Nhat Hanh recounts his mother's death and his coming to terms with it. After more than a year of mourning, he had a dream one night and realized she was with him everywhere. She was alive in him. She was alive in the trees, the grass, the clouds, the sky. Thich Nhat Hanh learned the lesson Jesus was teaching two thousand years ago in his parable of the wheat: *Truly, truly, I say to you, unless a grain of wheat falls into the earth and dies, it remains alone; but if it dies, it bears much fruit.* (John 12:24-26) He learned that when we die, it means only that the conditions for this life have changed and we will be manifested in some new way. All of those who have passed before us are here — in the trees, grass, the clouds, the sky.

turnip soup with turnip greens & bacon

This dish is a shining example of our cooking philosophy. There are only seven ingredients in the dish, counting the salt, but if these seven ingredients are put together correctly and with care, the soup is amazing. Not "amazing" in the sense of mind-spinning complexity, but in the totality of its simplicity. Turnip is what you will taste, and that's the whole point. The bacon is there to act as a balance, to offer some relief, much like an acid would do in a buerre blanc.

1 pound fine white turnips with their greens
1 onion
$3/4$ cup butter
1 tablespoon salt
1 quart milk
6 slices bacon
olive oil

The idea is to **chop** the hard vegetables finely so they'll cook as quickly as possible. This goes for all hard vegetables, whether fennel, carrots or rutabaga — the longer you cook them, the less flavor they will have.

Cut the turnips and the onion into medium-sized pieces and chop in a food processor until very fine.

In a 4-quart saucepan, melt $1/2$ cup butter over low heat. Once the butter is melted, add the turnip/onion mixture. Stir in the salt, cover and cook slowly for about 12 minutes. Make sure you stir it every 3 minutes or so to keep from browning, which will ruin the color of the soup.

After 12 minutes, add enough milk to just cover. Bring to a boil, then reduce the heat to a simmer and cook for 5 minutes more.

Purée in batches in a blender. Add the rest of the butter and adjust the seasoning. Keep warm.

for the turnip greens and bacon:

Put the bacon and a small splash of olive oil in an 8-inch frying pan and turn the heat to medium. The touch of oil will get the bacon started, plus add a little extra for sautéing the greens.

While the bacon is cooking, chop the turnip greens into $1/2$-inch pieces. Once the bacon has crisped nicely, add the greens and a little salt. Turn the heat up to almost high and sauté the greens until they're tender.

to serve:

Divide the soup into bowls and place a good portion of the sautéed greens and bacon in the middle of each serving.

YELLOW ON YELLOW ON YELLOW ON WHITE

A FEW YEARS AGO I was looking through a cookbook by a Japanese chef trained in France. The book was entirely in Japanese, so I was only able to look at the pictures. And what pictures they were! Every plate was perfect. So simple. So clean. To this day I have cherished one dish from that book as the most perfect I've ever seen. It was a terrine of yellow peppers with a sauce of yellow peppers and olive oil. There it was, a round white plate with a yellow terrine of many layers of yellow peppers in yellow aspic lying on top of a yellow sauce. I hope to some day produce a dish that captures that pure simplicity.

The artist Hans Hoffman has said, "The ability to simplify means to eliminate the unnecessary so that the necessary may speak." To me, the essence of perfect food is the elimination of everything except that which is necessary, and the true talent of a chef should be judged not by what she adds to the dish, but what she leaves out. A chef must know when to stop. It's too easy to add more and more stuff to a dish; it takes real talent, courage and self-confidence to serve a yellow pepper terrine with yellow pepper sauce and not find it necessary to add a garnish of a different color to break up the plate.

Where does this simplicity come from? Well, it's certainly not a new idea. Escoffier, over 100 years ago, was concerned about simplicity in food. Fernand Point preached it while commanding the stoves at La Pyramide, and the whole nouvelle cuisine movement took simplicity as a driving theme. Each generation of chefs must redefine what simple food means, but the fact that each generation is concerned about what "simple" means is telling.

Does our desire for simplicity in cuisine come from the fact that we live more and more complicated lives? Or is it hardwired into our genes from the days when we gathered nuts and berries? I don't know. I do know, however, that when I taste a tomato and it tastes like a tomato, I am happy.

—E.P.

roast pheasant
with cauliflower salad & bread sauce

This dish is based on some pretty classic ideas. First, we're going to roast the breast and braise the legs. Nothing fancy, but still the best way to cook a pheasant. Second is the bread sauce. We're not sure how long bread sauce has been around, but we think God was still in diapers when it was first introduced. Lastly, in classic French cuisine, and in particular during those really long, long meals, a simple salad is served with the roast. We will always have a soft spot in our cooking for the classical way of doing things. We like how it grounds our cooking and keeps us pointed forward.

The preparation of the pheasant is divided into legs and breast.

1 whole **pheasant**
1 onion, cut in a small dice
1 carrot, cut in a small dice
1 rib of celery taken from the heart,
    cut in a small dice
1 piece bacon cut into $^1/_4$-inch pieces
peppercorns
1 bay leaf
2 sage leaves
2 tablespoons butter
$^1/_4$ cup good Calvados
1 cup chicken stock

$^1/_4$ pound butter, cut into $^1/_4$-inch squares
$^3/_4$ cup chicken stock

2 cups milk
$^3/_4$ cup bread crumbs
1 shallot, peeled and kept whole

1 head cauliflower, cut into $^1/_2$-inch florets
$^1/_4$ cup raisins, plumped in hot water
$^1/_2$ cup **watercress**
1 tablespoon fresh chervil, chopped
rice vinegar
olive oil

We love **watercress**. Our first summer at the restaurant, we looked for a local source without much luck. Sometimes we could find it at the farmers market, but we couldn't find a regular source to rely on. One day towards the end of summer, I kvetched to our lunch cook Abraham about how frustrated I was, and he said his mom had tons of the stuff growing in the stream behind her house. "Excuse me?" I said. "Yeah, she doesn't know what to do with it all," he went on. Well, let me tell you, we quickly found something we could with it. For the next couple of months we were getting fresh, wild watercress on a daily basis. You can't get much more local than that. —E.P.

for the legs:

Preheat the oven to 320 degrees.

Remove the legs from the carcass without disturbing the breast.

In an ovenproof frying pan just large enough to hold the legs, place the diced vegetables, bacon, a couple of black peppercorns and the bay leaf. Season the legs with salt and drop them in on top of the vegetables. Melt 2 tablespoons of butter and spoon it over the legs. Add the sage leaves and tightly cover the pan with its lid, or use foil if there is no lid. Cook in the oven for 1 $^1/_2$ hours, basting every 15 minutes with the butter and juices that gather in the bottom of the pan.

After 1 $^1/_2$ hours, uncover and pour in the Calvados and chicken stock. Turn the heat up to 400 degrees and cook uncovered until the legs brown.

Technically this cooking method is not braising but *poële*. *Poële* is a French method that roasts entirely in butter; braise is a method in which the meat is cooked entirely in a liquid.

Remove the legs from the pan and set aside, keeping them warm.

Strain the sauce through a cheese cloth or napkin and let it set for a few minutes. Remove any fat that rises to the top.

for the breast:

Preheat the oven to 400 degrees.

Season the pheasant inside the cavity hole with salt and pepper. Ever so carefully, make a pocket between the skin and meat on each side of the breast. Divide the butter in half and stuff the pockets.

Put the breast in an oven-resistant frying pan and roast for 35 minutes, **basting** every 10 minutes with the butter that collects on the bottom of the pan. Check the doneness by piercing the fattest part of the breast against the center cartilage with a meat thermometer; the temperature should read 135 degrees. When you take it out of the oven, the breast will continue cooking and will reach about 140-143 degrees, which is the perfect temperature.

Put the breast on a plate and keep warm. Now, pour the fat out of the pan and put it on the stove on a medium flame. When the pan is good and hot, add the chicken stock, letting it boil down to ¼ cup. Add in the reserved cooking liquid from the legs and adjust the seasoning. Make sure the breast has rested for 20 minutes before carving. Keep the carcass to make stock or a nice soup.

Many recipes call for a pheasant breast to be covered with bacon slices to keep it from drying out. We've found that drying can be avoided by frequent **basting in** a moderate oven. Of course, the butter is also helping to keep the breast moist, but the absolute most important thing is to not overcook it. Pheasant should be cooked to medium and no more.

for the bread sauce:

Bring the milk to a boil. Add the crumbs, a pinch of salt and the shallot. Turn the heat down and simmer for 12 minutes. Discard the shallot. Whip the sauce with a whisk to smooth it out. Adjust the seasoning.

a note on pheasants

IF YOU'RE LUCKY ENOUGH to have wild pheasant available where you live, then you'll want to hang the bird in a cool, dark, dry place for about ten days before cooking. Keep the feathers on and the guts intact. Just tie a string around the head and let it dangle from a hook. Make sure that if you're hanging more than one bird, you allow space for the air to circulate between them.

Hanging game birds is extremely important for the finished product as it does two things: 1) It allows the meat to break down some, making it tender. 2) A fresh game bird will not have a very developed flavor and hanging fixes this problem.

The longer the bird hangs the stronger the flavor will be. Some Frenchmen we know will only eat the bird after the head separates from neck and the body falls to the floor. That's a tad long for us but you get the point.

The usual term applied to hanged birds is "high." For example, you can ask your supplier, "How high should a pheasant be before cooking?" Before cooking, you will of course pluck the feathers and remove the innards, setting aside the heart, liver and gizzard. We've included a good recipe for Pheasant Spread that uses these and which can be served with the pheasant.

for the cauliflower salad:

Do this while the pheasant is cooking.

Fill a 6-quart pot ⅔ full of water and season with 1 tablespoon salt. Place on high heat and allow it to come to a boil.

In the meantime, put some ice in a medium-sized bowl and add a little water.

As soon as your pot boils, add the cauliflower and cover with a lid to get it back to boiling as quickly as possible. Cook the cauliflower for 1½ minutes, then scoop it directly out of the pot and into the ice water to stop the cooking. When the cauliflower cools, take it out of the water and let it drain on a towel. Pat off any excess water. In a bowl, mix the cauliflower, raisins, watercress, chervil, a pinch of salt, some pepper and a splash of vinegar. Add enough olive oil to moisten the salad.

to assemble the dish:

Remove the thighs from the pheasant legs — leaving the drumstick bone — and place them in a hot oven to warm.

Remove the breasts from the carcass and slice into long, thin slices.

Take the thighs out of the oven and cut them into 4 equally-sized portions.

Divide the breast and leg meat and the salad among the plates, putting a good-sized dollop of bread sauce beside the breast.

pheasant spread

2 teaspoons butter
reserved pheasant liver, heart, and gizzard,
    all finely minced — keep the liver
    separate from the heart and gizzard
1 shallot, finely minced
2 teaspoons brandy or Cognac
1 tablespoon mustard
1 tablespoon parsley, finely chopped
3 tablespoons olive oil
4 ½-inch slices baguette bread

Melt the butter in a 7-inch pan over medium heat. Add the chopped gizzard, heart and shallot. Season with salt and pepper and cook, stirring, for 6 minutes. If the pan looks dry, add a little more butter. At the end of 6 minutes, turn the heat to slightly above medium-high and cook for another minute. Add the liver and cook, while stirring, for 2 minutes more. Turn off the heat. Add the Cognac, mustard, parsley and mix well. Spoon into a bowl and set aside.

Slice the baguette into 1-inch rounds. In a clean 7-inch pan, heat the olive oil over medium. Sauté the baguette slices on both sides until they are golden brown.

to plate:

Enjoy the spread with a glass of Rhone, Syrah or Bordeaux.

LIFE IS ALREADY TOO **COMPLICATED**

I AM BECOMING more and more convinced that one of the most important trends in the future will consist of doing as little as possible to food. The days of complex, over-worked food will come to an end. The next generation of cooks will take a carrot and let the carrot tell its story. They will take a beautiful, grass-fed piece of beef and simply cook it properly. Perfectly grown peaches will be served as they are, with little adornment.

In past days, cooks had to manipulate food. They had to serve heavy sauces. They had to present ingredients in complicated ways because, to put it bluntly, the meats, vegetables, fish and fruits were in bad shape because transportation was slow and refrigeration was poor. Today we know that is no longer the case.

I did an interview the other day concerning the various ways to use fresh cream and summer fruits. Throughout the interview, the reporter kept wanting me to talk about complicated desserts. He wanted me to give ideas that were difficult. I kept coming back to simple ideas that simply *presented* the fruits and cream. Why would we want to fold this and that, add some of the fruit, then toss and cut and shape the mixture when what we have is already nearly perfect? Why not *present* that beautiful strawberry — that perfect fruit that we only see for a few very short weeks in June — and celebrate its flavor? I would rather pair that amazing strawberry with some other equally amazing item (like fresh cream) and call it a perfect day. If those who dine with us at the restaurant learn one thing from me it's this: *Life is already too complicated to eat complicated food.*

—E.P.

warm indian creamed rice with pomegranates & pistachios

This is a variation of a classic East Indian dessert that is made on special occasions.

1 quart milk
$1/3$ cup short grain rice
1 inch piece of whole cinnamon
1 clove
3 cardamom seeds, gently ground; don't make a powder out of it
6 tablespoons sugar
$1/2$ cup pomegranate seeds
$1/2$ cup pistachios
2 tablespoons orange water

I hate **cloves**. I can't put into words my loathing for this foul creature. I include it only, and I mean *only*, because it is found in traditional recipes. —E.P.

Bring the milk to a boil in a 2-quart pot. Remove it from the heat, dip out a $1/2$ cup of the liquid and reserve.

Give the rice a good washing in a colander and add it to the milk still in the pot. Put the milk and rice mixture back on low heat and cook, stirring, for 20 minutes. Add the cinnamon stick, clove and cardamom. Cover the pot and continue to cook on low heat for 1 hour, stirring the rice every 15 minutes.

Wait, we're not done: add the sugar and the pomegranates and cook for another hour. At this point you'll need to keep a close eye on the pot. Continue stirring every 15 minutes. If it starts to get too thick or stick to the pan, add a splash more milk from the reserve.

Make sure you pitch the **clove** as far from the kitchen as you can and ask forgiveness from the cooking gods for using it. —E.P.

When that second hour is finished, remove the cinnamon stick and the clove.

Stir in the pistachios and orange water. Now, spoon the rice mixture into four bowls and let it cool down completely. We personally don't like this chilled. Give it a taste and choose what suits you.

9 Jen's daughter and I have a tea party one sunny Sunday. We brew a pot of tea and eat cookies. She draws me pictures of butterflies, aliens and germs while talking about Hannah Montana. Ah, is this not happiness?

winter

Winter, with its grey skies, brings out the introspective in us. Since business is at its slowest during these long months, we often let the cooks come in late and we take care of dinner prep ourselves.

If truth be told, these are our favorite times in the kitchen: just the pots, the storm outside, the thoughts inside.

christmas dinner

chestnut & oyster stew

salad of mâche, pomelo & christmas cactus flower

roast duck stuffed with onions & juniper berries,
served with roasted turnips & apples

traditional plum pudding

new year's eve

foie gras in brioche with pear compote

velouté of sunchokes with hazelnuts & parsley

sautéed walleye with great lakes caviar &
champagne sauce

short ribs braised in red wine and star anise
with potato purée & baby leeks

white & dark chocolate trifle

comfort food

classic french onion soup gratinée

roast chicken

braised winter greens

buttermilk biscuits with bacon & cheddar cheese

dried fruit cobbler

four of our favorite stews

daube of venison with mashed potatoes

cassoulet

wild boar ragout with root vegetables,
curly kale & cavatappi pasta

braised veal cheeks with cabbage, raisins & potatoes

christmas dinner

chestnut & oyster stew

salad of mâche, pomelo & christmas cactus flower

roast duck stuffed with onions & juniper berries,
served with roasted turnips & apples

traditional plum pudding

HOLIDAYS FIND US looking to tradition for inspiration, and
Christmas dinner is one of those times when we prefer to
keep the cooking toned down, sticking close to what is warm
and comfortable.

chestnut & oyster stew

2 pounds fresh chestnuts

1 medium onion, cut into small dice
1 medium carrot, cut into small dice
sprig of thyme
2 cups chicken stock
2 cups heavy cream
2 cups whole milk
20 fresh oysters, shucked from their shells

leaves from a celery heart

The **slashes** in the sides of the chestnuts allow steam to release during roasting. They also keep the nuts from exploding all over your oven.

Preheat oven to 400 degrees.

With a knife, **mark an X** on the flat side of each chestnut and place them on a cookie sheet. Roast for 40 minutes, then allow to cool until you can handle them easily. Peel, making sure to remove both layers.

In a 10-inch sauté pan, melt a walnut-sized nugget of butter over medium heat. Stir in the onions, carrots, thyme and season with salt. Continue sautéing until the onions are soft and translucent. Pour in the chicken stock and turn up the heat to high. When the stock has reduced to about ½ a cup, pour in the cream and milk. Add the chestnuts and simmer 5 more minutes, then add the oysters and cook for a quick 45 seconds. Adjust the salt and add some pepper.

to plate:
Ladle the soup into bowls and sprinkle with the celery heart leaves.

10

It's early in the morning and I walk into my kitchen. There are no sounds. The hood isn't on yet. There are no people talking or making noise. It's only me. I slowly begin putting together my workstation while thinking quietly about the day ahead. Ah, is this not happiness?

salad of mâche, pomelo & christmas cactus flower

4 handfuls mâche
1 or 2 pomelos
4 Christmas cactus flowers (Make sure these have
    not been sprayed with pesticides.)
1 shallot, chopped very small
mixed fresh herbs, chopped
olive oil
hazelnut or walnut oil
verjus or rice vinegar

Be careful with these **nut oils**. They can take over the salad if not used prudently. Remember that subtlety is the mark of great cuisine.

Wash and dry the mâche. Peel the pomelos carefully using a paring knife, then cut the fruit into segments. Remove the petals from the cactus flowers.

In a bowl, mix the mâche, pomelos, shallot and herbs. Drizzle in enough olive oil to moisten the leaves, a bit of the nut oil, a little verjus and a pinch of salt.

Plating salads requires a light hand. Pushing and mushing will result in a lifeless-looking salad. Give the leaves a little lift as you put them on the plate. Show them some love.

to plate:
Divide the salad on the **plates** and sprinkle with the flower petals.

a word on plating food:

PLATING FOOD IS often made more difficult than necessary. We have this idea that the plated dish has to be this complicated hodge-podge of garnishes, slices, precise placements and what not. Nothing could be further from the truth. Ask yourself: what is the purpose of plating food? Its purpose is simple: to make it possible to eat the food at the table. That's it, nothing more. We artfully arrange food on the plate to make it appealing to the eye before we start eating, but this can be taken too far. If a plate has too many details on it, or is too contrived, it may make diners wonder how many hands were on the food before it got to them. Also, taking too much time to plate a dish will ensure it makes it out to the guest cold.

Our approach to plating is the same as our approach to cooking. We want it to appear as natural as possible, with no extra garnishes or adornments or fancy tricks. Put the food on the plate, make it look nice and serve.

Every cook does it differently. What is important is that the rules of composition are followed. We'd like to suggest that the reader study the rules of composition in painting to gain some helpful insights into plating food. Plating food cannot be a random process. Food always tastes better when nicely composed on a plain white plate.

WANDERING THE VENTURES OF THE PAST

TAKING PART IN A tradition is a great way to touch the past and those who came before us. Olaf Stapleton in his classic *Last and First Men*, says it most eloquently:

> We are concerned with the past not only insofar as we make very rare contributions to it, but chiefly in two other manners.
>
> First, we are engaged upon the great enterprise of becoming lovingly acquainted with the past, the human past, in every detail. This is, so to speak, our supreme act of filial piety. When one being comes to know and love another, a new and beautiful thing is created, namely the love. The cosmos is thus far and at that date enhanced. We seek then to know and love every past mind that we can enter. In most cases we can know them with far more understanding than they can know themselves. Not the least of them, not the worst of them, shall be left out of this great work of understanding and admiration.
>
> There is another manner in which we are concerned with the human past. We need its help …. We, who have now learnt so thoroughly the supreme art of ecstatic fatalism, go humbly to the past to learn over again that other supreme achievement of the spirit, loyalty to the forces of life embattled against the forces of death. Wandering among the heroic and often forlorn ventures of the past, we are fired once more with primitive zeal. Thus, when we return to our own world, we are able, even while we preserve in our hearts the peace that passeth understanding, to struggle as though we cared only for victory.

Tradition for tradition's sake makes us dead inside. Tradition for the sake of remembrance gives us the zeal to fight another day.

roast duck stuffed with onions & juniper berries, served with roasted turnips & apples

1 whole duck, excess fat and innards removed
1 onion, cut into quarters
3 fresh sage leaves
$^1/_4$ cup Madeira wine or sherry
2 cups chicken stock

2 turnips
1 sprig of thyme
2 apples
sugar
butter

Preheat oven to 400 degrees.

Wash and dry the duck. Stuff the onion and sage inside the cavity and truss the legs. Season all over with salt and pepper.

Place the duck in an ovenproof skillet or pan big enough to hold it. Roast for 25 minutes. Turn the heat down to 350 degrees and continue to cook for 20 minutes more. Keep an eye on the solids in the bottom of the pan; if they look like they're going to burn, add a small amount of water.

Allow the finished duck to rest on a serving platter. Place the pan in which you cooked the duck on the stove and turn the heat to medium-low. Deglaze with the Madeira and chicken stock, scraping the solids off the bottom of the pan. Pour the juices into a clean, 2-quart sauce pan and reduce on high heat until it measures 1 cup. Adjust the seasoning.

for the apples and turnips:

When you've lowered the oven temperature for the duck to 350 degrees, prepare the apples and turnips. Put a 12-inch square of foil in an oven-proof pan and place the washed, whole turnips in the middle of the foil. Drizzle some olive oil on the turnips and set a sprig of thyme on top. Form a package with the foil and place into the oven. Roast until done — this should take about 45 minutes to an hour. Remove from the oven, open the foil package and allow the turnips to cool. Once cooled, cut into eighths.

Core and cut the apples into eighths. Toss the apple in 2 tablespoons of sugar and sauté in a 12-inch pan with 1 tablespoon butter over medium-high heat until golden brown. One minute before the apples are finished, add in the turnips. Stir for 1 more minute. Place the apples and turnips in a serving dish.

to serve:

Carve the duck at the table. Serve with a spoonful of the apples and turnips and drizzle the sauce over the duck.

A CROWN OF THORNS FOR THE PLUM PUDDING

PLUM PUDDING'S ORIGINS can be traced back to the 15th century, though possibly it is even older. By the middle of the 17th century, plum pudding was associated with Christmas. As its name implies, it was originally made with plums, or more specifically, prunes. As time went on, new fruits were brought to England from faraway lands and made their way into the pudding. Nowadays, it is a rare recipe indeed that includes prunes.

In its early days, plum pudding was served at the beginning of the meal and its recipe included minced meats. For a time in Puritan England, it was illegal to make because of its richness. As tastes changed, the meats were omitted and the dish found its way to the end of the meal. Traditionally, brandy is poured over the pudding and it is set alight and brought into a darkened dining room with great pomp and everyone cheering. Sometimes coins are baked into the pudding and the finder is assured of good luck and fortune in the coming year.

Tradition tells us that the pudding is to be made five weeks before Christmas. Technically, it's a good thing to give it plenty of time to develop its flavor. Some families actually make the pudding one year in advance.

It is religious tradition that calls for the five weeks advance preparation. According to this tradition, the pudding is made the 25th Sunday after Trinity (which is the Sunday after Pentecost), using thirteen ingredients which stand for Christ and his twelve disciples. The Sunday on which the pudding is made is called Stir-Sunday because each person in the family takes a turn stirring while making a wish. The stirring must be done in an east to west motion to symbolize the coming of the Wise Men from the East. The traditional garnish is a branch of holly, which stands for the crown of thorns Christ wore at his crucifixion.

traditional plum pudding

Make this pudding at least 30 days before you plan to serve it.

$1/2$ cup rum
1 peeled apple, cut into small dice
2 cups golden raisins
2 cups black raisins

$1/2$ cup dried bread crumbs
$1/2$ cup dark stout beer
3 eggs

1 pound beef suet, chopped very fine
(Suet is available from any butcher.)
$1/4$ cup candied orange rind
$1/4$ cup candied lemon rind
$1/4$ cup grated fresh ginger
1 cup chopped almonds

zest of one orange
juice of one orange
zest of $1/2$ lemon
juice of $1/2$ lemon
$1 1/3$ cups powdered sugar
$1/2$ teaspoon ground cinnamon
$1/2$ teaspoon ground nutmeg
$1/4$ teaspoon ground allspice
$1/4$ teaspoon ground mace
1 cup milk, scalded

$1/3$ cup rum, Cognac or brandy
2 cups whipped cream

Four days before you plan to make the pudding, place all the fruit to soak in the rum. Cover.

On baking day, heat oven to 250 degrees.

Stir the bread crumbs into the rum and fruit mixture. Stir in the stout. Add the eggs and mix well. Add all the rest of the ingredients except the additional rum and whipped cream. Stir well, making sure everything is well moistened with no dry spots.

Spoon the mixture into a buttered 10-cup bowl or pudding basin until it is $2/3$ full. Butter a large piece of parchment paper and secure it to the top of the bowl with kitchen string. Set the bowl inside a pan filled with at least 3 or 4 inches of water. Poach the pudding in the oven for 6 hours. Keep an eye on the water level and add more hot water if needed. Refrigerate the cooked pudding, with parchment paper in place, until 2 hours before you're ready to serve it.

On the day you plan to serve the pudding, remove it from the refrigerator and warm it in a pan of water in a 250 degree oven for 2 hours. Remove the parchment. The pudding will come out easily from the bowl. Place on a serving platter.

Whip the cream.

to serve:
Gently warm the rum, Cognac or brandy and pour it over the pudding. Set the pudding alight and present it to your guests in a dark dining room. Serve whipped cream on the side.

new year's eve

foie gras in brioche with pear compote

velouté of sunchokes with hazelnuts & parsley

sautéed walleye with great lakes caviar
& champagne sauce

short ribs braised in red wine and star anise
with potato purée & baby leeks

white & dark chocolate trifle

IT WAS THE dead of winter with a foot of snow on the ground when
we served this New Year's Eve menu at the restaurant our first year.
All the ingredients, except for the foie gras, were available locally.
It goes to show that if you dig hard enough where you live, you can
produce amazing food even when the forces of nature are against you.

foie gras in brioche with pear compote

Prepare the dough and the foie gras roll the day
before you plan to serve it.

4 cups flour
$^1/_4$ ounce dry yeast (This is equal to one
    envelope in most yeast packages.)
2 teaspoons salt
9 teaspoons sugar
6 eggs
2 tablespoons milk
$^3/_4$ pound butter, well softened

1 large raw foie gras
$^1/_4$ cup brandy
6 - 8 pieces thinly sliced bacon
4 quarts chicken stock

3 pears
$^1/_4$ cup Port
6 tablespoons sugar
1 tablespoon red wine vinegar
$^1/_2$ stick cinnamon

for the brioche:

Make the starter by placing 1 cup of flour in a pile in a bowl. Form a
shallow well in the top, add the yeast and $^1/_4$ cup tepid water. Starting with
the edges, mix the flour into the liquid until a soft dough is formed. With
a knife, cut a couple slits into the surface, cover the bowl with a towel and
set in a warm place to ferment for 2 hours.

Using a mixer with a dough hook, mix well on medium speed the salt,
sugar, 4 eggs, milk and 8 tablespoons of butter. Slowly add the rest of the
flour until a compact dough is formed. Continue kneading the dough for
2 minutes more. Add another egg and mix thoroughly. Add the last egg
and mix thoroughly. Add the remaining butter little by little until fully
incorporated. Lastly, pour in the starter and mix until smooth. Scrape the
dough into a bowl and set in a warm place to rise for a total of 10 hours. At
the halfway point, punch the dough down.

for the foie gras:

Separate the two lobes. Take out any veins. Put the lobes into a bowl and
douse with the brandy and place in the refrigerator to marinate for an
hour, turning the lobes over every 20 minutes.

Place the pieces of bacon side by side on a thin kitchen towel, slightly overlapping each strip. Season with salt and pepper. Lay the lobes of foie gras together over the bacon. Form the foie gras into the shape of a sausage, then roll the bacon around the lobes and tightly wrap with the towel. Tie both ends of the towel with kitchen string to form a tight package. Leave one of the string ends a little long so you can hang the roll after it is cooked.

Heat the chicken stock to 160 degrees and poach the foie gras and bacon roll — yes, inside the towel. After 4 minutes, remove the roll from the stock, and using the long end of string, hang it from one of your refrigerator racks until completely cool. You will want to place a plate underneath the roll to catch any drippings. Once cool, remove the foie gras roll from the cloth.

If you were to go through this whole process with the foie gras, leaving off the bacon, you would have a preparation known as Foie Gras au Torchon. It is one of the best ways to eat the delicacy.

to assemble and cook:

You're ready to assemble when the dough has proofed 10 hours and the foie gras has cooled in the fridge. Generously butter a Le Creuset terrine or a bread pan measuring 10 inches by 3 - 4 inches by at least 3 inches high. Press a 1 ½-inch layer of brioche dough into the bottom of the pan. Place the foie gras roll in the middle of the dough. Add another layer of brioche and secure it well to the bottom layer, sealing the foie gras inside. Set in a warm place for a couple hours until it has risen.

Preheat oven to 360 degrees.

Brush the top of the dough with egg yolk and bake until the crust is nice and brown. Let the bread cool before turning it out of the pan.

for the pear compote:

Place all the ingredients in a 2-quart sauce pan. When it comes to a boil, turn it down to a simmer. Cook for 20 minutes, then mash lightly with a fork. Allow to cool.

to finish the plate:

Slice the foie gras brioche into desired thicknesses — we like slices of about ⅜ inch. Place each slice on a plate and top with a rounded spoonful of compote.

velouté of sunchokes
with hazelnuts & parsley

This is one of our all-time favorite soups. We love the flavor of sunchokes, and the play they have with the hazelnuts and parsley is a delight.

5 cups chicken stock
$1/2$ pound butter
1 cup flour
2 pounds sunchokes,
    a.k.a. Jerusalem artichokes
1 egg yolk
$1/4$ cup heavy cream

$1/2$ handful roasted and peeled hazelnuts
parsley

for the soup:

Velouté is one of the 5 mother sauces in classic French cuisine. The name means "velvet," referring to its texture when made correctly. Velouté also makes a perfect base for many fine soups, including this one.

Bring the stock to a boil in a 6-quart sauce pan.

In another 4-quart sauce pan, melt $1/4$ pound of the butter. Whisk in the flour and cook, stirring constantly, on medium heat for 1 minute. Make sure the roux stays pale, as any color whatsoever will turn this delicate soup the wrong color. Now, pour the boiling stock into the roux and whisk quickly to keep any lumps from forming. Reserve the stock pan. Turn the heat down and simmer for 15 minutes. Set aside.

jerusalem artichokes

THE JERUSALEM ARTICHOKE is not from Jerusalem, nor is it an artichoke. It's a species of sunflower and was cultivated by Native Americans who called it "sunroot" long before any Europeans arrived. So what happened? Good question. First, for the name: When Europeans were first introduced to the plant, they gave it the Italian name *girasole*, which means sunflower. Over the years, the sound of the name morphed into *Jerusalem*. The artichoke misnomer came from Samuel de Champlain. He sent some samples back to France with the comment that they tasted much like, you guessed it, artichokes. Nowadays, cooks often refer to Jerusalem artichokes as "sunchokes," or even go back to the original name: sunroots.

In a food processor, mince the sunchokes. (It is possible, but not easy, to do this by hand.) In the stock pan, add 2 tablespoons of butter and melt over medium-low heat. Mix in the minced sunchokes and a dash of salt. Cover and let stew for 8-10 minutes, stirring to keep it from burning to the bottom of the pan.

Add the velouté to the sunchokes and return to a simmer. Cook an additional 8-10 minutes. Wash the 6-quart pan.

Purée the soup in batches in a blender to obtain a smooth texture.

Return the soup to the 6-quart pan and stir in the cream and the rest of the butter. Adjust the seasoning.

Just before serving, bring the soup back to a boil, then return to a low simmer. In a small bowl, mix the egg yolk with ¼ cup of the soup. Pour the contents of the bowl back into the soup and let simmer on very low for about 30 seconds. Do not allow the soup to boil as it will cause the yolk to curdle and form egg lumps.

for the hazelnuts:
In food processor put the hazelnuts, a handful of parsley, a pinch of salt and a small splash of olive oil. Process until a semi-chunky mixture is formed.

to plate:
Divide the soup into bowls and put a dollop of the hazelnut mixture on top.

I realize one evening during a busy dinner service that anytime I am in the kitchen, in the midst of my boiling pots, hot ovens and the controlled chaos that lives there, I am always more at ease than at any other time. I pause for a moment, take a deep breath and turn to plate the next dinner. Ah, is this not happiness?

sautéed walleye with great lakes caviar & champagne sauce

This dish is intended to be an appetizer in a longer menu. However, it can also make an excellent entrée by including vegetables—perhaps asparagus, grilled green onions, some sautéed or braised greens. If you wanted to include a starch, buttered potatoes would be best.

2 tablespoons butter
$^1/_2$ shallot, chopped
$^1/_2$ cup + 2 tablespoons good
        Champagne or sparkling **wine**

2 cups heavy cream
1 ounce Great Lakes caviar
        (Substitute any good quality caviar.)

olive oil
4 4-ounce fillets of **fresh walleye**,
        skin on

See p. 79 about cooking with **wine**.

A couple of things here: First, always use **fresh** fish. Fish that has been frozen completely changes taste and texture when it's thawed and cooked. Fish is a delicate food and must be treated in a delicate manner. Freezing is a violent process in general, and it is even more violent when applied to fish. Don't buy the line that anything can be "fresh-frozen." It's either "fresh" or "frozen" and cannot be both no matter what anyone tells you. Second, **walleye** is one of the best tasting freshwater fish around. It has a clean, mild, sweet flavor with a small flake. When eaten fresh there is no other freshwater fish that can match it.

for the sauce:

In a 2-quart saucepan, melt the butter over medium heat. Add the shallot and cook for 1 $^1/_2$ minutes, being careful not to let it brown as it will discolor the sauce. Add $^1/_2$ cup of the Champagne and turn the heat to high. Reduce to about a tablespoon.

Add the cream. (If you add the cream when there is too much wine left it may curdle.) Reduce again until the cream coats the back of a spoon. Season with salt.

to cook the fish:

Cooking fish is not an easy task. Here we are going to sauté. To sauté fish requires a good pan and hot oil. We recommend using a nonstick pan, like enamel-coated cast iron from Le Creuset.

Score the skin on each fillet and place skin down on paper towels. Allow to rest until the skin is dry; dry skin will crisp when it's cooked.

Season the meat side of the fish with salt and get a 12-inch frying pan hot over high heat. You will need to cook two fillets at a time in 2 batches.

Rule #1 in fish cookery: never crowd the pan.

12 We've been planning a surprise birthday party for my wife for months, and she's been led to think that the party on the books is for someone else. She doesn't realize that we've closed the restaurant for her. We've invited 40 or more of her friends. On the day of the event, there is plenty of wine and food. A local musician plays on the lawn outside the restaurant. As she rushes in, thinking she's late because of all the people milling around, we yell, "Surprise!" Ah, is this not happiness?

Pour about a tablespoon of olive oil into the frying pan. When the oil is good and hot, slide in the fish fillet, skin side down. Cook until the fillet is about ¾ done on one side. You can tell by the whitish coloring on the sides of the fish. Flip it and cook for another 30 seconds. Remove the fillets from the pan onto a warm plate. Repeat the process for the other 2 fillets.

to serve:

Just before serving, whisk another 2 tablespoons of Champagne into the sauce. The raw Champagne will re-enforce the Champagne taste. The caviar can also be added at this point, or you can keep it out of the sauce altogether, placing a rounded spoonful on top of the fish when you're ready to serve.

Put a pool of the sauce in the middle of the plate and arrange a fillet on top. If you are going to put the caviar on the fish, now is the time to do it.

This is a very simply presented dish. There is a white sauce, some black caviar and a golden brown piece of fish, ideally served on a spotless white plate. We think it would be a shame to put anything else on the plate. What we have before us is a dish that is elegant in its simplicity. Simplicity is our cooking mantra in general, and this applies to our plate presentations. Do no more than what is necessary to the plating. If it doesn't need a garnish, then don't use one.

SISYPHUS AND THE COOK

ONE OF THE GREAT CHEFS in the latter 20th century was Marco-Pierre White. A brilliant cook, he took the quest for perfection as far as one could, then hung up his apron. In his autobiography, *The Devil in the Kitchen*, he explained: "The nonstop process of refining dishes and striving for perfection was exhausting. I didn't want to push myself anymore. Even when you have three stars, you still have to keep raising your game. People look at you as the top chef and their expectations become greater. It's all about taking yourself as far as you can. It can seem never-ending."

The last sentence is what caught my attention. Why do chefs put themselves under so much pressure to perform? Why are they willing to spend so much time away from their families and friends in their pursuit? How can we explain their relentlessness in the face of such an unattainable quest?

I've spent some time thinking and have finally found my answer in the myth of Sisyphus. Sisyphus is a prideful character from Greek mythology who was condemned to an eternity of rolling a boulder up a steep hill only to have it roll back down again as soon as he reached the top. Albert Camus points out that the real test was not in rolling the stone up the hill, but the time spent walking back down the hill to begin his appointed task anew. Camus believed Sisyphus was happy; he wrote, "I leave Sisyphus at the foot of the mountain! One always finds one's burden again. But Sisyphus teaches the higher fidelity that negates the gods and raises rocks. He too concludes that all is well. This universe henceforth without a master seems to him neither sterile nor futile. Each atom of that stone, each mineral flake of that night-filled mountain, in itself forms a world. The struggle itself toward the heights is enough to fill a man's heart. One must imagine Sisyphus happy."

The cook who pursues perfection is much like the anti-hero Sisyphus. He has a task ahead of him that will never find completion. And I believe it is the *task* that is important, not the *goal*. In spite of the fact that we can never cook the perfect dish, we cook anyway. And, for the most part, I am happy with that.

—E.P.

short ribs braised in red wine and star anise with potato purée & baby leeks

8 pieces of short ribs about 4 inches in
    length
leek greens
$^1/_2$ carrot, chopped into small dice
1 stalk celery, chopped into small dice
1 head garlic, broken up but with the skins on
3 star anise
1 bottle Cabernet Sauvignon
2 sprigs thyme

2 Idaho potatoes, unpeeled
$^3/_4$ - 1 $^1/_4$ cups hot milk
$^3/_4$ - 1 pound butter, cut into small cubes
    and well chilled

12 baby leeks, or 1 mature leek
butter

for the ribs:

Season the ribs with salt and pepper. In a 12-inch frying pan, heat 3 tablespoons olive oil over medium-high. When oil is hot, add the ribs 2 at a time and brown on each side. Set aside.

Dice a cup of the leek greens and put them into the hot pan along with the carrots, celery and garlic. Cook for a few minutes until a little color appears on the vegetables — this will add both color and depth of flavor to the braise.

We suggest cooking the ribs in a crock pot. If you don't have a crock pot, then use a deep bottom pan that is at least 4 inches deep.

Place the ribs, cooked vegetables, wine, garlic, anise, thyme and enough water to cover the ingredients in a **cooking vessel** of choice. If you're using a crock pot, choose the all-day setting and come back in 7 hours. If you're using the oven method, then heat the oven to 275 degrees. Cover the pot tightly with its lid and put into the oven on the middle rack. It will need to cook for at least 5 hours, perhaps as long as 6. Check the liquid level about halfway through and add more water as necessary to keep the ingredients covered.

When the cooking is complete, carefully remove the ribs and strain the cooking liquid into a pot large enough to comfortably hold it. Let the stock stand for about 10 minutes to allow the fat to collect on top. Carefully skim and discard the fat. Dip out 1 cup of stock and reserve. Put the stock pan on the stove and turn the heat to medium-high. Reduce to 1 ¼ cups.

Discard the bones from the ribs. Taste and adjust the seasoning. Put aside and keep warm.

Cooking potatoes with
the skins on keeps them
from getting waterlogged.
Waterlogged potatoes
make a runny purée. For
an explanation of why you
need so much salt, see
page 32.

Also, don't let your
potatoes cool too much
before peeling, as this will
cause them to get gummy
when puréed.

for the purée:

Put the potatoes in a pot large enough to hold them and cover with water to at least 1 inch over the surface of the potatoes. Pour in ¼ cup of salt and turn the heat to high. When the water boils, turn the heat down but keep the pot boiling. A hard boil tends to break the potatoes up and you want them whole with the skins still on. The potatoes are done when a knife can be inserted easily.

Drain the water completely. Peel the potatoes while they're still hot, using a towel to hold them and a paring knife to peel them.

Push the potatoes through a food mill or ricer or mash as smoothly as possible and place in a pan large enough to hold them. On medium-low heat, start mixing in the hot milk a little at a time with a wooden spoon. Every ¼ cup or so, alternate with some of the chilled butter. Continue until you reach the desired consistency. Adjust the seasoning.

for the leeks:

Wash the leeks and place in a pan just large enough to hold them.

Cover with water and add a nugget of butter about the size of an olive and a little salt. Cook on high heat until the water evaporates and a nice sauce forms. Be careful not to reduce too much or the sauce will break and be greasy. See instructions on page 179 for saving a broken sauce.

to plate:

Put the ribs in a pan with the reserved cooking liquid and heat on medium until hot.

Spoon some potatoes into the middle of a plate and set 2 pieces of the short ribs on top. Spoon the sauce over the ribs and garnish the plate with 3 pieces of the baby leeks. (If you are using a large leek, you will need to cut the leek into quarters.)

white & dark chocolate trifle

7 eggs
12 ounces semi-sweet dark **chocolate**
4 tablespoons butter cut into cubes
$1/4$ cup powdered sugar
$1/2$ vanilla bean
$1/3$ cup dark chocolate liqueur, eg, Bailey's

4 ounces white chocolate
$1/3$ cup white chocolate liqueur
the other $1/2$ of the vanilla bean
8 ounces mascarpone brought to
        room temperature
1 cup cream

1 cup cream
2 tablespoons sugar
cocoa powder
fresh nutmeg

The **chocolate** we use comes from chocolatier Mimi Wheeler, a resident of Empire, Michigan, just a few miles to the west of us. She only buys certified fair-trade chocolate from Ecuador. Like all of the artisans who call northern Michigan home, Mimi is passionate about her chocolate and it shows in the final product.

to make the cake:

This flourless chocolate cake is wonderful all by itself, served warm in wedges with a little sweetened whipped cream.

Preheat oven to 350 degrees.

Fill a 4-quart sauce pan halfway with water and bring to a boil. Reduce to a simmer.

Lightly butter a 10-inch springform pan.

Put the eggs, still in their shells, in a bowl and cover with hot water from the tap. Warm eggs make for bigger volume when whipped.

Over the pot of simmering water, melt the butter and dark chocolate in a medium bowl. While the chocolate is melting, whip the eggs and the powdered sugar until they triple in size. Scrape the seeds out of one of the vanilla bean halves and add to the chocolate mixture, along with the dark chocolate liqueur. Mix well. Remove from the heat and fold in the beaten eggs.

Spoon the batter into the springform pan and bake for 30 minutes. Let cool before turning out of the pan.

for the mousse:

Put the white chocolate, white chocolate liqueur, ¼ cup of water and the seeds from the other half of the vanilla bean into a medium bowl and melt over the pot of simmering water. When the chocolate melts, mix well with a whisk, then gradually add the mascarpone. When all of the ingredients are incorporated, remove from the heat and allow to cool.

Whip 1 cup of cream to medium peaks and fold into the cooled mousse.

to assemble:

Cut the entire chocolate cake into ¼-inch slices — you should have at least 12 slices. From each slice, cut a 3-inch circle. (Save the scraps to eat with your morning coffee or tea.) Whip 1 cup of cream with the sugar until it forms a nice saucy consistency.

Spoon a pool of whipped cream into the middle of a plate. Place a cake round on top of the cream, then a dollop of mousse, then another cake round. Do this until you have three cake rounds stacked up with mousse in the middle. Put a dollop of the mousse on top of the stack. Sprinkle cocoa powder on top and a bit of freshly grated nutmeg. Repeat for all 4 plates.

13

Drinking tea out of a pretty tea cup.
Ah, is this not happiness?

PEOPLE HAVE BEEN ASKING Jen and I about the creative process chefs go through. If the truth be told, Jen is the more creative of the two of us; set her down for ten minutes and she can rattle off idea after idea. I, on the other hand, will not even talk to a client about a possible dinner unless Jen is with me. I have a terrible time coming up with ideas off-the-cuff. It's much more productive for me to wander around a market. That's just how my mind works.

During one of our first meetings with the publisher and the editor of this cookbook, the topic of creativity came up. I insisted that food be simply prepared and kept as close to natural as possible. Heather, our editor, reminded me that I talk about pairing foods together and learning to "taste" them in our heads. I know rabbit and chocolate go together, and I know rabbit and tomatoes go together, so with this knowledge I was willing to bet that chocolate and tomatoes would go together even though the combination may take some tweaking.

Well, I was called to task about this. Heather wondered if "tweaking" contradicted my insistence on "simple" and "natural." I don't think so. "Natural" means not forcing the dish to do something it doesn't want to. When I say "natural," I mean it in the Taoist sense: *wu wei*, to do without doing. Basically, it means allowing things to happen on their own, following the flow of the moment without getting in the way.

Here is the process I used to come up with a dish that has both chocolate and tomatoes in it, but doesn't force them together. If I were to force the idea, I might come up with something like Tomato Ice Cream with Chocolate Sauce — not very appetizing. Instead, I started with the idea of pairing tomato and chocolate and let it flow from there.

I scribbled down my idea process and it looked something like this:

chocolate	chicken
basil	nuts
tomato	cherries
pepper	salt
chili pepper	tarragon
vinegar	onions
vanilla	

That was my starting point — a list of the things I knew went with both of the main ingredients. Then, I sat back and started thinking. What is "natural" about this list? For me (but not necessarily for you), four items stood out: chili peppers, chicken, cherries and nuts. I knew all four went well with my idea of chocolate and tomatoes and would make a great bridge. Okay, now I had some structure. There was most definitely a dish here … But where?

It sounded to me like some kind of mole, but I didn't really want to re-create a classic. I wanted something I could call my own. (Though, chefs borrow from the classics all the time: they give us a platform from which to jump.)

A picture of what I wanted the dish to look like began to form. I saw a bowl with some stewed tomatoes with sliced onions. It's somewhat of an abstract picture, but it's a starting point.The chicken would be braised with the chocolate, cherries (I will use dried ones for this dish because the braising is a long, slow process) and chili peppers. This part was easy. Then, I thought, it's a Mexican-inspired dish, so how about a Mexican beer for the braise? Since I try to use local ingredients, I'd try to find a local beer.

The main part of the dish completed: the tomatoes were stewed and the chicken was cooked with its parts. Now to plate it. Again, I let this happen naturally. I wanted to use the braising liquid because it would be a waste not to. I scrapped using the tomato broth and used the braising liquid instead. So as not to waste the tomato broth, I'd pour it into the braising liquid and reduce the whole until I got what I was looking for in taste and consistency.

Then I thought, What if I toasted some pumpkin seeds and puréed them into the sauce? This would be as good as using nuts and a little different, though there might be a texture problem. Would puréed seeds be too grainy? No, if I used a blender, it would make a nice smooth purée — and I had to admit the toasted seeds would add a nice dimension to the whole dish.

Now I had a bowl of stewed tomatoes with some braised chicken thighs resting nicely on them. A sprinkle of cilantro would tie the whole thing together.

There you have it, Heather, chocolate and tomatoes together in a natural, unforced way: Chicken Thighs Braised with Chocolate, Chili Peppers and Dried Cherries, Served with Stewed Tomatoes. (See the recipe on page 23.)

— E.P.

comfort food

classic french onion soup gratinée

roast chicken

braised winter greens

buttermilk biscuits with bacon & cheddar cheese

dried fruit cobbler

IT'S SNOWING OUTSIDE. You're not sure if the thermometer is broken or if it really *is* five below zero. What you do know is that it's cozy in the house. It's one of those lazy Sunday afternoons with a hot pot of tea, a good book, perhaps a fire and a lit pipe. Days like these don't clamor for fancy food. Days like these yearn for heart-warming fare that thumbs its nose at the storm outside.

classic french onion soup gratinée

We've made hundreds of gallons of this soup and still can't get enough of it. Oddly, however, it's one of those dishes that too many cooks make incorrectly. We've seen recipes call for everything from soy sauce to Worchester sauce to balsamic vinegar. Others want the onions to cook until they all but fall apart. All this extra stuff makes a simple and satisfying dish way too complicated. It's really very easy to make and requires only a few ingredients, some patience and a hot oven.

$^1/_3$ pound butter

3 yellow onions, sliced with the grain of
    the onion then cut into 1-inch lengths
    (This is to make it easier to eat the soup
    with a spoon. There is nothing worse than
    onion dribbling down your chin.)

$^1/_2$ handful flour

1 cup red wine

2 sprigs thyme

7 cups chicken stock

olive oil

8 slices of day-old baguette, sliced
    to $^1/_2$ -inch thick

8 slices of **cheese**

The traditional **cheese** is a French cheese called *Comte*. You can also use Gruyere, Emmental or Swiss cheese. Some American-made cheeses that would also fit the bill are: Roth Kase's Grand Cru Gruyere or Upland's Pleasant Ridge out of Wisconsin. Here in Michigan, Grassfield's Edam. Don't use provolone or mozzarella as they're much too rich and get stringy. The Swiss/Gruyere style cheeses offer a bite that counters the oniony richness of the soup.

for the soup:

Put the butter into a 4-quart pan and melt over medium-low heat. Add the onions and season with salt and pepper. For the next 30 minutes, let the onions cook slowly. *Slowly* is the key word here. If you cook them too quickly, their natural **sweetness** won't come out.

    Sweat the onions, making sure to stir frequently with a wooden spoon, especially after all the water has evaporated. The onions will not begin to color until all that liquid is gone, and you'll have to pay close attention so they don't burn to the bottom of the pan. Your attention will be rewarded though, once the onions start to turn a beautiful, **golden brown**.

Sometimes you'll see sugar called for in an onion soup recipe; this is because the recipe is asking you to cook the onions too quickly, thus missing out on the onions' natural **sweetness**, and even inviting a hint of bitterness. But, if cooked correctly—and by correctly we mean *slow, patient cooking* — then no sugar is needed. Mom would be proud.

The color of the onions is very important. Too little color (too white) and the flavor will not develop correctly; your soup will be characterless. Too much color (very brown) and the flavor will be too strong. **Golden brown** is the color you're looking for. Golden brown gives you a rich, mellow soup.

Once you have the right color, sprinkle in a half-handful of flour while stirring with the wooden spoon. Basically, what you're making is a *roux*, a classic French thickening agent. Only add enough flour to lightly coat the onions — you don't want to make wallpaper paste. Stir in the red wine, add the sprig of thyme and finally, the chicken stock. Turn up the heat to bring to a boil, then turn down to a simmer. Simmer for 30 minutes. Adjust the seasoning.

for the croutons:

In an 8-inch frying pan, pour enough olive oil to fill the bottom to a ¼-inch. Turn the heat to medium-high. When the oil is hot (you can check this by dipping a corner of your sliced baguette in the oil to see if it fries) fry 4 pieces at a time until golden brown. Turn the slices over and fry on the other side until golden brown. Do this for all the bread. Drain the croutons on a paper towel.

to finish:

Preheat oven to 450 degrees.

Ladle the soup into 4 8-ounce, ovenproof cups, leaving ¼-inch at the top. Put two **croutons** on top of the soup.

Over the croutons, place 2 slices of cheese, making sure to crisscross them so there are 8 corners showing, not 4. Place the cups on a baking tray and bake in the oven for about 15 minutes, or until the cheese is nice and brown and bubbly. Serve the hot cups on napkin-covered plates. (The napkin keeps the cup from moving around on the plate.)

You may need to get creative fitting these **croutons** in the bowl. Sometimes they are just too big and you'll need to break one up. The important thing is that the croutons cover the entire top of the soup. Don't break them up so small that you end up with crumbs.

The best way to transfer the soup cups hot from the oven is to fold a towel into a long strip and use it like an oven mitt with each end for each hand. Sometimes the cheese will drip down during baking, sticking the bowl to the pan; a gentle twist of the cup will loosen it.

THERE'S SOME CONTROVERSY over what's actually "classic" in this recipe. For example, some say you have to use beef broth for the soup to truly be "classic." Some say the wine must be Port. There's no real consensus on the matter no matter how far back you go. These days, Joel Robochon uses chicken stock, and since he's one of the best chefs of the 20th century I am willing to bet it's okay. Personally, I like chicken stock because it doesn't overpower the soup, thus allowing us to better taste the onions.

—E.P.

roast chicken

A chef's true test of talent is found in two dishes: the quality of her consommé and the tastiness of her roast chicken. Fortunately, there are as many ways to roast chicken as there are cooks. Here's ours.

1 whole chicken: 5-6 pounds, preferably
    organic and free range
$1/2$ pound butter, cut into large squares
1 large onion, cut into quarters
3 fresh sage leaves
$1/4$ cup Madeira or sherry
1 cup chicken stock

Preheat oven to 450 degrees.

Remove any giblets from the chicken's cavity. (Keep them, discard them, do what you like with them. Maybe you could flour the liver and gizzard and fry them up.)

Rinse and dry the bird, then season the chicken inside and out with salt and pepper.

Carefully push your finger under the skin of each breast and make a pocket. Insert the butter squares into the pocket, packing it tightly. If you need more butter, use more butter. The butter keeps the breast from drying out and provides flavor.

Stuff the onion and sage into the cavity and truss the chicken.

Set the bird on its back in a roasting pan and place in the oven. After 15 minutes, turn the heat down to 400 degrees. Cook for 45 minutes, checking the temperature at 35 minutes to be safe. To check the temperature, insert a meat thermometer between the thigh and breast until you hit the joint of the leg. We prefer to take the chicken out of the oven when the temperature reads 140 degrees. It will continue to cook outside the oven, reaching about 145, which is a perfectly cooked chicken.

Two things here:
1) You always want to **stuff** the cavity of any bird you roast, whether it's chicken, duck, grouse, squab or pheasant. Why? To keep the breasts from cooking too quickly. If the cavity is hollow, the heat will cook the meat inside and out. Putting something in there — in this case, onions — slows down the heat intake from the underside of the breast, making it possible for it to cook in the same amount of time as the legs.
2) Trussing the bird — again, you should do this with all roasted birds. Trussing keeps the bird compact, ensuring it will cook evenly.

Here is where we have a major disagreement with standard temperature charts. Almost every chart out there will tell you that chicken is only done when the internal temperature reaches 165 degrees. Are you kidding? The health department says 165 degrees because they know the crap coming from the giant processors can be dangerous and needs to be cooked for a long time to kill whatever diseases those poor birds might be carrying. But if you use small producers — producers that, of course, are inspected by the proper authorities — then you shouldn't have to cook the bejeezus out of the bird.

Resting the meat is vital because it allows all the juices, which have rushed to the middle, to re-distribute throughout the meat. Cutting into meat that hasn't rested tells the story: all the juice pours out on the plate, leaving the meat high and dry.

Carefully transfer the chicken to a platter large enough to hold it. Allow it to **rest** for at least 20 minutes.

Pour out any grease in the roasting pan. If you did your job right, there will be some browned bits and pieces stuck to the bottom of the pan.

Place the roasting pan on the stovetop over medium heat and get it hot without burning the fond. As soon as it's hot, pour in the Madeira and stock and start scraping the bottom of the pan using a wooden spoon. Turn the heat to high and reduce until you've got ¾ cup. Adjust the seasoning. Pour into a dish and reserve.

This is called a *fond*, which is the French word for "base" or "foundation." Although in cooking, fond generally refers to stock (the chicken stock you'll use in this recipe is called *fond de volaille*), this fond is the basis of the sauce you're about to make.

to finish:

Simply carve up the chicken and serve the sauce on the side.

a word on chickens

THE ATROCITIES PERPETUATED in giant meat-packing and processing plants are unforgivable. These factories are set up for one purpose only: to push as many animals as possible through their system in a given 24-hour period. There is no care for the quality of the product or for compassionate treatment of the animals (nor, sometimes, of the human workers in the plants). Moreover, the animals found in these plants were often raised under the most horrific of conditions. Conditions that affect the well-being of the animal go on to affect the quality of their meat and the health of the consumer.

At The Cooks' House, we get our meats from eight different ranchers and farmers. Our chicken comes from a farm just south of us. The birds are treated with genuine consideration and allowed to live in open spaces. When we cook one, we can taste the love — the flavor is magnificent and the meat is tender. Remember, a cook can never make up for inferior product, no matter how talented she is.

braised winter greens

1 tablespoon olive oil
$1/2$ onion, sliced with the grain
2 cloves garlic, peeled and sliced
3 stalks Swiss chard, cut into 2-inch pieces
3 stalks green kale, cut into 2-inch pieces
    with the stems discarded
3 stalks mustard greens, cut into 2-inch
    pieces with the stems discarded
1 cup chicken stock

Put the olive oil into a 2-quart pan along with the onion and garlic. Season with salt and pepper. Add the greens and sauté for about 3 minutes over medium heat, or until they're well wilted. Add the chicken stock and continue to cook for 4 minutes more. Adjust the seasoning. Serve in its own bowl.

buttermilk biscuits
with bacon & cheddar cheese

Buttermilk biscuit recipes are often passed down from generation to generation, and we don't believe in re-inventing the wheel. For this basic recipe, we've turned to the amazing book by James Peterson called *Cooking*. It's a must-have book for all cooking libraries. What we did do, however, was take the basic Peterson recipe and modify it.

2 cups flour
$1/2$ teaspoon baking soda
$1 1/2$ teaspoons baking powder
$1/4$ teaspoon salt
6 tablespoons cold butter, sliced into 12 pieces
4 slices bacon, cooked crisp and crumbled (our addition)
$1/3$ cup shredded cheddar cheese (our addition)
$3/4$ cup buttermilk or more, as needed

Pre-heat oven to 400 degrees.

In a bowl, stir together the flour, baking soda, baking powder and salt until well mixed. Put the butter on top of the flour mixture, then cut through the mixture with a pastry blender until the butter is about the size of peas. Add the bacon and cheese and mix with a wooden spoon. Pour in the buttermilk and, using a wooden spoon, combine until the liquid has been absorbed and there is no loose flour in the bottom of the bowl. If you still see loose flour, mix in another 2 tablespoons buttermilk to absorb it. Be careful not to over-stir the dough or you'll get tough biscuits.

Dump the dough onto a work surface and gather it together into a mound with your hands. Knead it long enough so that it holds together in a shaggy mass. Flatten into a disk. Flour a work surface and roll out the disk to $2/3$-inch thick. Using a round, 2 $1/2$-inch biscuit or cookie cutter, cut out as many disks as possible and arrange them on an ungreased sheet pan, spacing them about 1 inch apart. If you like, pull together the trimmings, reroll and cut them out the same way.

Turn down the oven to 375 and bake the biscuits for about 20 minutes, or until golden brown. Allow to cool on a rack for 10 minutes. Serve while still warm.

dried fruit cobbler

2 cups mixed dried fruits
1 1/4 cups cherry juice (We're from cherry country; we
      can't help ourselves. If you can't find cherry juice, feel
      free to substitute another type of fruit juice.)
1 1/4 cups Port
1 tablespoon molasses
2 cups sugar
1 cup flour
1 teaspoon baking powder
3/4 cup milk
4 tablespoons butter
2 cups sweetened whipped cream

Preheat oven to 325 degrees.

Combine in a 2-quart sauce pan the dried fruits, cherry juice, wine, molasses and 1/4 cup of the sugar. Bring to a boil, then reduce heat to a rapid simmer. Cook for 5 to 8 minutes. You want the liquid to turn into a medium-bodied syrup.

While the fruits are cooking, prepare the batter by whisking together the flour, baking powder, remaining sugar and the milk. Whisk thoroughly to get rid of all the lumps.

Put the butter into a 9- x 9-inch baking pan and place in the oven to melt. When it's melted, remove the pan from the oven and pour in the batter. Do not stir. Spoon the fruits evenly over the batter and pour in the leftover juice. Return the pan back to the oven and bake for 1 hour, or until an inserted knife comes out clean.

to serve:
Scoop onto plates and serve with whipped cream.

It is wintertime and a storm is raging outside. The restaurant is warm, but because of the storm we have no customers. I'm sitting at the table beside our big window, occasionally looking outside while reading a cookbook and drinking tea. Ah, is this not happiness?

14

PEANUT BUTTER AND JELLY

LAST NIGHT, NOT SURPRISINGLY, I got hungry around 2:00 a.m.
As I often do in such cases, I opened the refrigerator door and stood there
waiting for some inspiration. Nothing. So I closed the door, got a glass of
water and reopened the door, hoping something had magically appeared in
my absence. Nothing.

In times like these, the ol' pb&j comes to the rescue, a perfect food if
ever there was one. Two slices of bread, a layer of peanut butter (creamy,
thank you very much) and a layer of jelly (actually, I prefer jam): heaven.

The peanut butter and jelly sandwich has a bad rap amongst foodies,
but if made with great bread, fresh peanut butter and homemade jam this
lunchtime standard takes on new meaning. Much of what we consider to be
mundane food is mundane simply because it has never been taken seriously
enough to be given proper attention and preparation guidance.

I love what Escoffier wrote in his 1907 *Le Guide Culinaire:*

"One can but deplore the arbitrary proscription which so materially
reduces the resources at the disposal of the cook ... and one can only hope
that reason and good sense may, at no remote period, intervene to check the
purposeless demands of both entertainers and their guest in this respect."

What constitutes "proper" food? If I am a lover of great cooking, does
this mean I can't partake in a peanut butter and jelly sandwich without
running the risk of the food police taking me to task? I like bean burritos
and baloney sandwiches also — does this mean I can't consider myself a
true cook? Frankly, I think the general public would be surprised at what
chefs eat when they're at home.

Much of what it means to cook is found in taking risks. It's easy to put
foie gras on the menu all the time, but I like it most when I see dishes
like cookies and milk. It says to me that this is a cook who thinks the
commonplace deserves some time in the limelight. The key, I think, is to
use great ingredients and make the food correctly. It doesn't matter what
the dish is called; what matters is how it tastes.

—E.P.

four of our favorite stews

daube of venison with mashed potatoes

cassoulet

wild boar ragout with root vegetables,
curly kale & cavatappi pasta

braised veal cheeks with cabbage, raisins & potatoes

WINTER IS THAT HARSH period in which life just seems to hang on, no more. But it is, in fact, during winter that life begins. Late winter is the time the seeds planted in warmer times take root and begin to grow.

We like late winter because of what's hidden under its surface. We may not appreciate it while in the middle of yet another storm, but when the sun shines and we hear the birds of spring sing, we're able to look back with a weathered eye and know that winter was the beginning of spring.

The following recipes are surely the definition of "slow food." Most of them require a few hours to prepare, one of them needs more than two days. But "slow" is what makes them inviting. We think it's hardly a coincidence that winter foods often take longer to cook than summer foods. Winter has a way of stretching out time, and it seems that the foods we eat during this time of year take on the same characteristics.

daube of venison with mashed potatoes

A classic French *daube* is made with cheap cuts of meat, red wine, carrots and herbs left to stew all day over the hot embers of an open hearth. While most of us don't have open hearths to cook on, we can still get excellent results.

4 $1/2$ to 5 pounds venison shoulder, cut into
    1 $1/2$-inch cubes
2 bottles good red wine
1 sprig thyme
1 bay leaf
a couple sprigs parsley, just the stems
6 slices thick bacon, cut in half lengthwise and
    blanched in boiling water for 2 minutes
3 carrots, cut into $1/4$-inch rounds
2 onions, cut into medium dice
1 head garlic, broken up into cloves, peeled
    and cut in half lengthwise
1 orange peel, no bitter pith
    (Use a vegetable peeler.)
1 **pig trotter,** cut in half lengthwise
    (Your butcher can do this.)
a handful of flour

3 medium-sized russet potatoes
$1/4$ cup salt
1 to 2 cups hot milk
a couple tablespoons chilled **butter**

Pig trotters are one of those long forgotten, olden-days ingredients. The truth is, they're so good that where still served they're often the main course. In classic French cuisine, they're boned out and rubbed with strong mustard, breaded and fried — my mouth is watering just thinking about it. Trotters also have a lot of gelatin, and that gelatin will give the daube a body that can't be obtained any other way.   —E.P.

Fernand Point, father of modern French cuisine, used to say, "**Butter!!** Give me butter!!" We have to agree.

Remember, the quality of **wine** you use will directly affect the quality of your dish. Cheap wine makes a finished dish taste cheap. We're not advocating breaking into that '61 Chateau Latour you've been saving, but we would like to see you spend more than the cost of a tube of toothpaste.

for the daube:

Season the venison with salt and pepper and marinate in the **wine** with the thyme, bay leaf and parsley stems for at least 6 hours; overnight is best.

Preheat oven to 220 degrees.

Drain the venison, reserving the wine. Splash 1-2 tablespoons olive oil into a heavy pot with a well-fitting lid and turn the heat to high. When the oil begins to smoke, start adding the venison. Brown in 3 or 4 batches, pouring out the spent oil and starting with fresh each time.

When all the venison is browned, change the oil one last time, turn the heat down to medium, and brown the bacon, vegetables and garlic.

Return the venison to the pot, along with the marinating wine, orange peel and pig trotter. If you need to, add enough water to cover the meat.

Now this is the fun part: Put a handful of flour on a table and add enough water to make a thick paste. Shape a rope from the dough, long enough to fit the lip of the pot. Set the dough in place, put the lid on and press to seal.

When the daube comes to a boil, place in oven and leave it to cook for the next 5-6 hours. Don't look at it, don't think about it and don't mess with it.

One hour before the daube is finished, make the mashed potatoes.

for the mashed potatoes:
In a large pot, put the potatoes and enough water to fully submerge them. Add a ¼ cup of salt. (Yes, that's a lot of salt. Trust us and see page 37.) Bring the potatoes to a boil then reduce the heat and cook until a knife can be inserted easily. Drain the water completely. Peel the potatoes while they're still hot, using a towel to hold them and a paring knife to peel them. Push the potatoes through a food mill, ricer or mash as smoothly as possible and place in a pan large enough to hold them. On medium-low heat, start mixing in the hot milk a little at a time with a wooden spoon. Every ¼ cup or so, alternate with some of the chilled butter. Continue until you reach the desired consistency. Adjust the seasoning.

to present:
More fun here: Carefully take the daube from the oven and put the pot on a plate on top of a napkin. (The napkin will keep the pot from slipping around, plus it looks nicer.) Walk the pot and the mashed potatoes to the dining room. Using the back of a knife, carefully break up the crust and remove the lid. You may have to use a spoon for leverage to pop it off. Also, make sure you remove the lid in a way that directs the steam away from you. Steam burns are some of the nastiest you can get. Ladle the daube into bowls along with a good scoop of potatoes.

15 Watching a small child pick up his food with his fingers and stick it on the fork before putting it in his mouth. Ah, is this not happiness?

cassoulet

This is a two-day tour de force. The French really outdid themselves when they created this masterpiece.

4 (2 if they are large) legs of duck confit (Recipe follows.)

1 pork hock (Beware: don't get a smoked pork hock.)
2 beef short ribs (Yes, I know, beef is not traditionally
    found in cassoulet, but we like it.)
1 lamb shank
1 onion, left whole, peeled
3 bay leaves
2 sprigs thyme
1 gallon chicken stock
4 cups beans, soaked overnight or for an hour
    in boiling water (These beans can be cannellini,
    cranberry, navy or great northern.)
20 slices bacon
4 sausages, anything but breakfast sausages
$^1/_2$ cup dry bread crumbs

for the confit:

Season the duck legs with salt and allow to set for at least 6 hours.

Preheat oven to 225 degrees.

Place the legs in a pot large enough to hold them and cover with duck fat — olive oil will also work. Cook in the oven for 4 hours, or until the meat falls easily off the bone. Cool the legs without removing them from the fat. If the legs are completely submerged in oil, they will keep in the refrigerator for up to 6 months.

classic cassoulet

THERE ARE THREE SCHOOLS of thought as to what goes into true cassoulet, and each school will argue their position with passion. The three camps are as follows: 1) Cassoulet contains mostly pork, 2) Cassoulet is made with lamb only, 3) Cassoulet is made with anything. I'm in the third camp. In my mind the only ingredient required to make cassoulet is beans. Everything else is up for grabs. I like the everything-but-the-kitchen-sink approach — but not for any cultural or philosophical reasons. The reason is simply because this approach gives me the most wiggle room. I like sausages, duck, pork, lamb, chicken, beef (gasp) and all sorts of things in my cassoulet and often will throw in whatever is available at the moment. In France, cassoulet is such a serious dish that certain regulations must be followed if one wants to serve it. But don't get hung up in silly arguments. Just make the damn thing, sit back and enjoy it. —E. P.

for the cassoulet:

Season the hock, short ribs and lamb shank with salt and pepper and place, along with the whole onion, in a large pot. Cover with the chicken stock. Bring to a simmer and cook for the next 2-3 hours, or until each piece of meat is tender. The different meats will finish cooking at different times, so take each piece out when done and set aside on a platter. Make sure the meats in the pot are always covered with liquid—you will probably have to add water. When the meats are done, you'll have a fabulously flavored broth, and if we did our job right, there will be enough of this broth to serve either as a first course or alongside the cassoulet.

Add the soaked beans to the broth and bring to a boil, then simmer for 30 minutes. Again, if you need to, add some water to keep the broth level up. Drain the beans, reserve the broth.

to assemble:

Preheat the oven to 275 degrees.

In a cast iron Dutch oven, or a casserole dish large enough to hold everything, completely line the sides and the bottom of the dish with the bacon strips. Spoon in half the beans. Put all the meats — including the sausage — on top of the beans and cover with the remaining beans, then pour in the broth until it just covers all the ingredients. Sprinkle the dry bread crumbs evenly over the top and drizzle the confit fat over this. Put the pot (uncovered) in the oven and cook for the next 2 hours, occasionally breaking up the crust.

So now that it's in the oven, the big question of how many times the crust needs to be broken comes up. We've heard staunch proclamations from cassoulet aficionados that the crust must be broken 7 times, no more, no less. Others say at least 4 times, and still others will say break the crust whenever the beans begin to look to dry.

We're in the 4-times camp with the emphasis on *whenever it needs it*. When the beans on top begin to look too dry, break up the crust with the back of a spoon and gently (emphasis on *gently*) press down on the crumbs, letting some of the liquid and a new layer of beans come up. If you have to, add a little of the reserved broth.

We must say that "breaking up the crust" is one of our favorite cooking rituals. The romantic in us (yes, there's a romantic even in Eric, but don't tell anyone, he has a reputation to uphold) comes out and we imagine ourselves in an old farmhouse kitchen with a group of friends, drinking and carrying on.

After 2 hours, take the cassoulet out of the oven and let it cool in the refrigerator overnight. This is a very important step in the process as it lets all those flavors mellow.

The next day, take the cassoulet out of the refrigerator and let it set on the counter for 45 minutes to an hour.

Preheat oven to 350 degrees.

Put the cassoulet back in the oven and let it heat up until it begins to bubble, about 1 hour. Turn the oven down to 250 and add enough water to cover the beans. Cook for 2 more hours, keeping an eye on the crust; you probably will only have to break it up once.

Now it's time to bring the French masterpiece to the table. Make a show of this. It's taken you two days to get this far and it deserves a celebration. Invite your best friends and have them bring plenty of crusty bread and wine. Hopefully, it's snowing like the dickens.

wild boar ragout with root vegetables, curly kale & cavatappi pasta

1 shoulder wild boar, cut into 1-inch pieces (If you can't get boar, a
    4-5-pound pork shoulder will be fine. We encourage you to try the boar,
    though, as it is more flavorful than pork and much more fun.)
1 bottle good Brunello, Barolo, Bordeaux or Côtes du Rhône
olive oil
2 large onions, cut into small dice
1 carrot, cut into $1/4$-inch rounds
2 celery stalks from the heart
2 handfuls of different kinds of root vegetables, cut into
    $1/2$-inch pieces (Celery root, parsnips, rutabaga, turnips, salsify, etc.)
1 head garlic, broken up and peeled
1 bunch curly kale
thyme
bay leaf
1 tablespoon good prepared mustard
1 pound cavatappi pasta
parmesan for grating

Season the boar with salt and pepper and marinate in the wine for at least 6 hours; overnight is best.

Preheat oven to 220 degrees.

Drain the boar, reserving the wine. Pour 1-2 tablespoons olive oil into a heavy pot with a well-fitting lid and turn the heat to high. When the oil begins to smoke, brown the boar in 4 different batches, changing the oil after each batch. When all the boar meat is browned, turn the heat down to medium; change the olive oil one last time and stir in the vegetables. Cook until slightly browned. Add the boar meat back in (plus any juices), as well as the thyme, bay leaf, mustard and reserved wine. Additional **water** may be needed to cover the meat.

Cover the pot. When it comes to a boil, place in the oven for the next 5 hours or so. Check the level of the liquid after about 2 hours, but unless it's very low — you'll want a nice, thick sauce in the end — leave it be.

Remove the ragout from the oven and carefully remove the lid. If the sauce is too thick, thin it out with a bit of water on the stove top until you get the desired consistency. (On the other hand, if the sauce is too thin, you can also reduce it on the stovetop.) Adjust the seasoning.

Cook the pasta in salted water.

to finish:

There are a couple of options here. One is to toss the pasta in butter, put it in bowls, spooning the ragout on top. The other is to stir the pasta directly into the ragout. Make sure to grate some parmesan on top of the ragout before you serve it.

Now, a valid question would be: *Why not use beef stock or other stock instead of **water**?* You could, and there would be nothing wrong with that, but the way we see it, the stew is going to cook for the next 5 hours or so, and the water you're adding now is going to be made into a stock by time it's finished.

TODAY'S QUIET REPOSE

TODAY, while taking a break from my usual hectic schedule, I was drinking a pot of tea and reading through one of my favorite books, *The Book of Tea*, by Okakura Kakuzo.

> *Tea began as a medicine and grew into a beverage. In China, in the eighth century, it entered the realm of poetry as one of the polite amusements. The fifteenth century saw Japan ennoble it into a religion of aestheticism—Teaism. Teaism is a cult founded on the adoration of the beautiful among the sordid facts of everyday existence. It inculcates purity and harmony, the mystery of mutual charity, the romanticism of the social order. It is essentially a worship of the Imperfect, as it is a tender attempt to accomplish something possible in this impossible thing we know as life.*

What I love most about those words is how they don't make excuses for the imperfections we find in everyday life, but in fact celebrate and raise them to a place of beauty and of art. Tea, as Mr. Okakura tells it, is all about finding what is possible in this life. Tea is victorious in its simple outlook!

I especially love Okakura's use of the word "tender" when referring to our attempt to find the possible in the impossible. Tender means *given to gentleness and sentimentality*, as one dictionary defines it. I actually read the word "tender" in this context as not pushing your way through life. To be tender is to see life as something that is fragile or easily hurt, and life, like a great cup of tea, is fragile and easily ruined if not made with care. The movement of life is subtle, and if we are tender with it we will find ourselves able to follow its movements and flow with them instead of battling against them. You could say that life, like tea, is easy enough to make. But to make either of them well it takes tenderness, and tenderness is something I find myself having to renew daily.

—E.P.

braised veal cheeks with cabbage, raisins & potatoes

Veal cheeks are one of the most under-utilized and most flavorful cuts of meat. The general rule of thumb is: the more a muscle moves, the better the flavor, and if you have ever watched a cow, all they do is stand there and chew. Those cheeks get quite the workout.

4 pounds veal cheeks
1 large onion, cut into small dice
1 carrot, cut into small dice
2 stalks celery from the heart, cut into small dice
1 head garlic, broken up into cloves and peeled
1 sprig thyme
2 bay leaves
2 teaspoons fennel seed, toasted in a dry pan over
    high heat until you can smell it (It's important to
    continuously shake the pan so the seeds don't burn.)
2 teaspoons coriander seed, same directions as above
2 cups white wine
2 cups chicken stock
4 slices bacon, cut into $^1/_4$-inch wide pieces
1 head cabbage cut into 8 wedges (Leave the core for this as
    it will hold the leaves together. Also, peel away the first 3 or
    4 layers of leaves.)
2 Yukon Gold potatoes, cut into $^3/_4$-inch dice
1 cup raisins

Preheat oven to 250 degrees.

Season the veal cheeks with salt and pepper, then heat 1-2 tablespoons olive oil over medium-high heat in a heavy-bottomed pot large enough to hold the meat and vegetables. Make sure it has a tight-fitting lid. When the oil just begins to smoke, add the cheeks and brown on both sides. Do this in batches, changing the oil after each batch. After the meat is done, turn the heat down to medium, change the oil once more and add the vegetables. Season with salt and sauté until they take on a little color. Add the garlic, thyme, bay leaf, fennel seeds and coriander seeds, cooking for about 1 minute more. Pour in the white wine and chicken stock (and water, if necessary), making sure the liquid covers everything. Cover the pot and put it in the oven for about 4 hours.

After 4 hours, remove the meat from the pot, reserving it on a plate. Pour the broth into a container large enough to hold it. Dry out the pot — no need to wash it — and put it on the stovetop over medium heat.

Add the bacon and brown. Once the bacon is browned, add the cabbage wedges, potatoes, raisins, a bit of salt and enough of the reserved broth to just cover. Simmer for 20 minutes.

Return the reserved meat to the pot, mixing it in with the cabbage. Simmer for 10 minutes more.

to serve:
Divide the meat among the bowls, along with a wedge or two of cabbage, potatoes and a good amount of the juice. Make sure you have plenty of bread on hand for sopping.

ODDS&ENDS

chicken stock

4 pounds chicken carcass: necks, wings, backs, all that stuff you trim off. Chop the pieces well, to get at all the good marrow and gelatin that's in inside

3 onions, chopped into small dice (If you want, and this is what we like, leave the skins on as this will give your stock a nice golden brown color. If you need a whiter stock, then don't include the skins.)

1 head garlic, cloves separated

10 or so sprigs of thyme

2 bay leaves

Put all of the ingredients into a 2-gallon pot and add enough cold water to just cover the bones. Cold water is essential because the impurities that can cloud the stock only dissolve in cold water. As the stock comes to a boil, fat and impurities will rise to the top. Use a ladle to skim this off and throw away. (There is something Zen-like in skimming stock and it is a process we always take great pleasure in performing.) As soon as the stock comes to a boil, turn it down to a slow simmer. This is a very important step in ensuring a clear stock. If it boils too quickly, the impurities and fat will recycle through the stock and cloud it. Cook it for no more than 4 hours. What we're doing is simmering to extract the flavor from the main ingredient, which in this case is meat and bones. With chicken, after 4 hours, you've definitely accomplished that. Fish stock should cook no longer than 30 minutes. Beef stock, however, takes a long time, about 18 hours.

When the stock has finished cooking, carefully strain it through a napkin, filter or cheese cloth.

LATE WINTER is the hardest part of the year for me. I'm tired of the snow and
I don't think I've been really warm since November. I've had enough of root
vegetables and would love nothing more than to see a garlic scape or morel. But
I have to be patient. I have to wait it out. I know there is green grass under those
three feet of snow and there are farmers in the area who will soon begin looking
for the first sprouts of spring.

I've spent the last couple of hours going through seed catalogs, looking at
what's available for growing in this region. We've had more than a few farmers
approach us for a list of items we'd like them to grow. I've put in my two cents and
now I pass the list to Jen and let her go to town. We want to keep incorporating
more and more heirloom vegetables into the menu. It's exciting thinking about
not just carrots, but Atomic Red Carrots; not just potatoes, but LaRatte potatoes;
not just run-of-the-mill hard squashes, but Uncle David's Dakota Dessert
Squash. What the hell is skirret? I don't know, but if someone grows it for me,
I'll use it with pride.

I think the number of fresh vegetables available in northern Michigan
will begin to plump up if we, and by *we* I mean *all of us who live here*, show the
farmers there is interest and sound reason behind making sure more products
are available. We do that by buying the items they're selling, even at the end of
winter. Do you want more variety? Then seed the future by buying locally now.

— E.P.

> The first cup of tea of the day.
> Ah, is that not happiness.

17

spring

The first day of spring
is one thing,
and the first spring day
is another.
—HENRY van DYKE

hot and cold

COLD SPRING MENU

purée of jerusalem artichoke soup with garlic confit

roast quail on polenta with dried plums

greek walnut-honey cake with earl grey ice cream

WARM SPRING MENU

stinging nettle soup with horseradish dumplings

new potatoes & white anchovies with vinegar onions

chicken legs stuffed with sausage, served with
porcini mushrooms & fava beans

tangerine mousse

easter

tatsoi & sorrel salad with pickled ramps,
boiled eggs & tarragon

seven hour leg of lamb with fava beans, peas,
savory & goat cheese gnocchi

peaches with cardamom & muscat

celebrating
heirloom vegetables

salad of butter crunch, flame & paris white lettuces
with tempura of fairy tale eggplant, upland cress,
chrysanthemum flowers & french breakfast radishes

platter of grilled bianca di maggio onions,
fresh sardines, swedish peanut potatoes, lemons
& fakir parsley root leaves

moong dahl with early snowball cauliflower
& bloomsdale long-standing spinach

charleston "ice cream"

charentais melon soup with homemade yogurt & mint

a fancy late spring lunch

salad of tender greens, crispy capers,
pancetta & almonds

soft shell crab, broccoli rabe & chipotle sandwiches

apricots poached with ginger & lime

hot and cold

COLD SPRING MENU

purée of jerusalem artichoke soup with garlic confit

roast quail on polenta with dried plums

greek walnut-honey cake with earl grey ice cream

WARM SPRING MENU

stinging nettle soup with horseradish dumplings

new potatoes & white anchovies with vinegar onions

chicken legs stuffed with sausage, served with porcini
mushrooms & fava beans

tangerine mousse

WAKING UP ON the first day of a northerly spring can feel like just another winter's day. The ground is still barren, there is nothing on the horizon. It's mornings like these when we find out what we're made of as cooks.

Early spring is a time of anticipation. And the menus of anticipation freshen up our palates and get them ready for the riches of what's to come.

The two menus in this chapter are made up of items available from two different climates. The first is from what we are able to get locally here in northern Michigan. The second is from ingredients that are available from warmer parts of the country.

purée of jerusalem artichoke soup
with garlic confit

Cold Spring Menu

2 heads garlic
olive oil

1 pound Jerusalem artichokes, washed thoroughly
    and roughly chopped with skin on
1 medium onion, roughly chopped
$1/4$ pound butter
milk
$1/2$ cup fresh cream

for the confit:

Break up and peel the garlic, but leave the cloves whole. In a pan just big enough to hold the garlic, pour in enough olive oil to barely cover. Cook at a very slow simmer for 30 minutes.

for the soup:

Place the Jerusalem artichokes and onion in a food processor and process until a very fine mince has been reached. Work quickly because these vegetables brown quickly when exposed to air.

Heat the butter in a 6-quart pan over medium-low. Add the minced vegetables and salt and cover. Let cook, stirring every minute or so, for 5 minutes. Add the milk and bring the soup to a boil. Lower the heat to medium and cook for 8 minutes more. Return the soup to the food processor in batches and **blend**.

Add the cream and adjust the seasoning.

to plate:

Ladle the soup into bowls. With a fork, crush 2 cloves of the garlic confit and place them on top. Drizzle a bit of the oil you used to cook the garlic over the surface of the soup.

Be very careful when **blending** hot liquids. Only fill the hopper half full and make sure you've replaced the top securely before turning it on so that the hot soup doesn't explode out of the top. How you turn the blender on is also important: don't just flip the switch to "high" as this may also cause an explosion. If you have a blender with a speed dial, start it on the lowest speed and slowly bring it up to high. If your blender only has a high/low switch, then the trick is to quickly flick the switch on and off a few times to get the soup moving.

roast quail on polenta with dried plums

3 slices bacon, cut into smallish dice and
　　blanched in hot water for 30 seconds
1 medium onion, cut into small dice
6 cups chicken stock
1 sprig thyme
1 cup coarse **cornmeal**
handful of aged white cheddar
　　cheese, grated
$1/2$ cup cream

8 semi-boneless quail
olive oil
1 tablespoon butter
4 sprigs thyme
1 shallot, chopped fine
1 cup dried plums
$1/8$ cup Madeira or sherry
2 cups chicken stock

Try not to use instant **cornmeal** as the texture is completely different from that of the longer cooking cornmeal. Also, the cooking times used in the recipe are for the longer cooking type. If you can only find instant cornmeal, then follow the recommended cooking times on the package.

for the polenta:

Preheat oven to 350 degrees.

In a 6-quart ovenproof pan, melt 1 tablespoon of butter over medium heat. Add the bacon and onions, seasoning with salt and a little pepper. Sauté until the bacon is crispy and the onions brown a little. Stir in 4 cups of the chicken stock, one sprig of the thyme and bring to a boil.

When the stock is boiling, slowly add the cornmeal while stirring with a wooden spoon. After all the cornmeal has been added, continue stirring until there are no lumps.

Put a lid on the pan and place in the oven. Cook for 35-40 minutes, stirring every 10 minutes or so to keep the polenta from burning on the bottom.

When the cornmeal is nice and creamy, take it out of the oven. Stir in 2 more tablespoons of butter, the cheese and the cream. Adjust the seasoning. Put the lid back on and keep warm.

for the roasted quail:

Turn the oven up to 450 degrees.

Season the quails inside and out. In an ovenproof **pan** large enough to hold all the quails, heat a tablespoon of olive oil over medium-high. When the oil is hot, add the quail breast-side down and sear until brown.

Turn the quails over and add 1 tablespoon of butter and thyme sprigs. Put the pan in the oven and roast for 6 minutes. Twice during roasting, baste the quails with the hot oil/butter from the bottom of the pan. Basting helps keep the quails from drying out. After 6 minutes, take the quails out of the oven and allow them to rest on a plate in a warm place.

Toss out any remaining oil from the pan. Over medium heat, add in a tablespoon of olive oil and the shallot. Sauté for 1 minute. Add the dried plums and cook for 30 seconds. Add the Madeira and 2 cups of chicken stock. Turn the heat up to high and reduce the liquid to 1 cup. Adjust the seasoning.

to plate:

Spoon a heap of polenta onto each plate. Place 2 quails per plate on top of the polenta. Spoon some of the sauce over the quails.

If at all possible, do not use a nonstick **pan**. During the roasting process we want a *fond* to form, and this will not happen with a nonstick pan. A fond is all the beautiful brown stuff that accumulates on the bottom of a pan whenever you cook meat. High in flavor, it's very important for the pan sauce at the end of the recipe.

a word on garnishing

TOO OFTEN we think we need to add a sprig, or a fancy vegetable or a sprinkle of something to a plate to make it look better. Our contention is if we have to garnish the plate to make it look better, then the plate wasn't constructed properly in the first place. Have you ever looked at a food picture, or been handed a plate at dinner and had trouble finding the main idea? It is our belief that a plate should garnish itself. Take this quail dish for instance: it's a plate of polenta with two quails and some sauce. The plate is perfect in its simplicity. The dish looks exactly as it should. A garnish would distract from its natural beauty.

Be confident in your food. Present it as it is and make no apologies.

greek walnut-honey cake
with earl grey ice cream

2 cups walnuts
1 cup all-purpose flour
1 teaspoon baking powder
$1/2$ teaspoon baking soda
$1/2$ teaspoon salt
1 teaspoon cinnamon, freshly grated
    on a microplane
3 eggs
$1/2$ cup dark **brown sugar**
1 teaspoon vanilla extract
1 teaspoon orange zest, use the microplane
$1/2$ cup salad oil
$1/4$ cup orange juice

1 slice lemon, $1/4$ -inch thick
$1/4$ cup honey
$2/3$ cup water
$1/4$ cup sugar

2 cups whole milk
8 egg yolks
1 vanilla bean, split and seeds scraped out, or
    1 teaspoon vanilla extract
$2/3$ cup sugar
3 tea bags of Earl Grey **tea**
$1 1/2$ cups heavy whipping cream

You can make your own **brown sugar** by adding molasses to regular sugar. That's how we do it at the restaurant. Stir in the molasses until you get the color you're looking for. Easy! Make just the amount you need and you'll never have a brown sugar brick in your pantry again.

We want to caution you on what is a *good* **tea** bag and what is a *bad* tea bag. *Good* tea bags are silken or nylon, holding whole leaves allowing plenty of room for the leaves to expand. *Bad* tea bags are those little paper things with the shredded leaves inside.

for the greek walnut-honey cake:

Preheat oven to 350 degrees.

    Butter a 10-inch cake pan.

    In a food processor, mix nuts, baking powder, baking soda, flour, salt and cinnamon until finely chopped and distributed.

    In a bowl, beat the eggs with an electric mixer for 3 minutes. You want the eggs light in color and thick in texture. After 3 minutes, begin adding the sugar and beat for 2 more minutes. Add the vanilla and zest. Turn the beater speed to high and add the oil slowly, just like you would if you were making a mayonnaise. Stir in the flour mixture and the orange juice.

Spoon the mixture into the cake pan and place on a rack in the lower third of the oven. Bake for 25 minutes. A finished cake should be springy to the touch and a knife inserted in the center should come out clean.

while the cake is baking, make the honey syrup:

Place lemon, honey, sugar and water in a pan on the stove and bring to a boil. Turn down to a simmer and cook for 5 minutes.

When the cake has cooled for about 15 minutes, spoon the honey syrup over the top. Allow the cake to soak in the syrup for a couple of hours before serving.

for the earl grey ice cream:

This should be made ahead of time, even the day before.

In a mixing bowl, whisk the egg yolks and sugar until a ribbon forms when the whisk is removed from the mixture.

Heat the milk, vanilla bean seeds and pod and the tea bags in a pan over medium heat until almost boiling. Turn off the heat and steep for 5 minutes. Discard the vanilla bean pod and tea bags.

Slowly stir a ¼ cup of the hot milk into the bowl — you don't want the yolks to curdle. Once this small amount of milk has "tempered" the mixture, add the rest. Wash out the milk pan and fill it halfway with hot water. Bring the water to a boil, then turn down to a simmer. Place the bowl of yolks and milk on top of the simmering water. Using a rubber spatula, stir the mixture until it coats the spatula. Don't let the water come to a boil again as it can cause lumps to form in the custard.

Now that the custard has thickened, take it off the heat. Stir it occasionally until it cools. Put the cooled custard into an ice cream machine and freeze. When the ice cream is half-frozen, lightly whip 1 cup of the heavy whipping cream and fold it into the ice cream. Continue to freeze until the ice cream has hardened.

to plate:

With 1 teaspoon of sugar, lightly whip ½ cup of whipping cream. Spoon a pool of the cream onto the plate. Place a piece of the warm honey-walnut cake on the cream and put a scoop of the ice cream on top.

stinging nettle soup
with horseradish dumplings

We love this soup because it takes what is harmful in nature and turns it into a nourishing meal.

fresh **horseradish** root
3 tablespoons vinegar

olive oil
1 large onion, halved, and each half
    cut into slices with the grain
2 sprigs thyme
$^1/_2$ pound **stinging nettle** leaves,
    chopped into $^1/_2$-inch pieces

1 $^1/_2$ quarts chicken stock
$^1/_2$ cup sour cream

4 teaspoons butter at room temperature
2 cups flour
4 teaspoons baking powder
1 cup milk

Be sure to use garden gloves when handling the stems of **stinging nettles**. Although it is usually sold "stemless," you should still be cautious. A little needle prick can cause you to break out in a rash.

for the horseradish:

Peel and finely chop 1 $^1/_4$ cups of the fresh horseradish. Place in a blender with enough water to barely cover. Add a pinch of salt. Puree, adding more water if needed, but not so much that you make it runny. Turn off the blender and add the **vinegar**.

for the soup:

Into a 3-quart pan, pour about 1 – 2 tablespoons of olive oil. Add the onion and thyme sprigs and sweat over medium-low heat until the onions are soft and translucent. Add the nettles, season with salt and pepper and turn the heat to medium-high. Sauté for about 2 minutes. Add the chicken stock and bring to a boil. When it boils, turn it down to a simmer and cook for 15 minutes. Add the sour cream and adjust the seasoning.

When you add the **vinegar** depends on how hot you want your horseradish. Wimps should add it straight away. Those who enjoy the mind-numbing experience of atomic hot should wait 3 minutes. Of course, any time in between is fine as well. The vinegar stabilizes the heat factor, setting it in stone.

for the dumplings:

Using a fork or pastry cutter, cut the butter into the flour until the mixture resembles coarse cornmeal. Add a pinch of salt and the baking powder and stir. Pour in the milk and a teaspoon of the prepared horseradish. Stir with a fork until a dough forms. Don't overdo it or you'll get tough dumplings. Drop the dumplings by the teaspoonful into the simmering soup. You should have enough dough for about 20 dumplings. Cook for 10 minutes.

To serve:

Ladle the soup into bowls, making sure to distribute the dumplings equally.

horseradish

MAKING PREPARED HORSERADISH at home is easy and tastes wonderful. Be aware though, that fresh horseradish can get strong when pureeing or chopping — don't inhale the fumes.

Only prepare as much as you think you'll use in a short amount of time. Freshly prepared horseradish will keep for about four weeks if stored it in a covered container. The whole root will keep several months in a plastic bag in the refrigerator.

I had a cook one time ask me if the horseradish was still good and, without giving me a chance, she pushed the jar under my nose. I got a nice big whiff of the stuff. My eyes turned inside out, my nose started to run, I coughed and gasped. I even forgot my name and I think I may have passed out for a few minutes. As soon as I recovered and was able to speak, I assured her it was still good and that I would appreciate it if she would never do that again. —E.P.

new potatoes & white anchovies with vinegar onions

Warm Spring Menu

This is one of those simple appetizers we so love. There's not much preparation involved, but the flavors are straightforwardly perfect.

1 $^3/_4$ cups rice wine vinegar
1 large red onion, cut into slices against the
    grain
$^1/_4$ cup olive oil

1 pound new potatoes
1 flat white anchovies (If white anchovies are not available, don't substitute with the brown ones commonly found on grocery shelves. Use smoked whitefish instead, or smoked trout.)

Fleur de Sel or Kosher salt
cilantro, picked down into small sprigs

Fleur de Sel is the end result of an exacting process that requires exact conditions. The best, and really the only true Fleur de Sel is found in Brittany, France. The process begins by filtering seawater through an intricate series of channels into large basins. Just the right amount of evaporation under the right conditions will form a crust on top of the water. The salty crust is then painstakingly hand-harvested with rakes. In the olden days the job was women's work because they supposedly handled the rakes more delicately than men. True enough, a clumsy rake will cause the salt to sink to the bottom of the water, ruined.

Do not cook with Fleur de Sel; sprinkle it onto food at the end of the cooking process for a wonderful salty crunch.

Never allow **potatoes** to sit in their cooking water as they'll take on a reheated flavor. Always pour the water off immediately after cooking, even if you don't plan on using them right away. To keep them warm, simply put a lid on the pot.

for the onions:
Warm the vinegar in a pan until it's just simmering — stay away from those fumes. In a bowl, stir the onions with the olive oil, then add the warmed rice vinegar. Let stand for 1 hour.

for the potatoes:
Boil the **potatoes** in water and a handful of salt until completely cooked but not mushy. Pour off the water.

to finish the dish:
In the pot, crush the potatoes gently until the skins begin to break. Place a large spoonful on a plate and flatten it out lightly. Sprinkle on some olive oil, a bit of the coarse salt and a crack of pepper. Dollop some vinegar onions on top of the potatoes. Make sure there's enough juice that it runs off the potatoes and onto the plate. Arrange a few white anchovies on top of and around the potatoes and onions. Garnish with a sprig of cilantro.

chicken legs stuffed with sausage, served with porcini mushrooms & fava beans

$^1/_2$ pound ground pork
3 cloves garlic, finely chopped
1 sprig rosemary, finely chopped
small handful of flat leaf parsley, finely chopped
$^1/_8$ teaspoon fresh nutmeg
white wine

4 boned-out chicken thighs and legs, leaving the
    thigh and leg in one piece
4 12-inch square pieces of aluminum foil

1 $^1/_2$ cups fresh fava beans, out of the shell

1 shallot, finely chopped
two medium or 1 cup fresh porcini mushrooms,
    sliced
$^1/_4$ cup sherry vinegar
$^1/_4$ cup plus a splash white wine
1 cup chicken stock

for the stuffing

Mix the ground pork, garlic, rosemary, parsley, nutmeg and a splash of white wine in a bowl. Set aside.

for the chicken:

Preheat oven to 450 degrees.

    Place the chicken skin-side down on a cutting board and season lightly with salt. In between the thigh and the leg, place a 2-ounce piece of the sausage stuffing rolled into the shape of a cigar. Fold the thigh over to cover the sausage. Season the outside of the chicken with salt and pepper.

    Sprinkle one of the aluminum foil sheets with olive oil and place a chicken piece in the center. Tightly roll the chicken in the foil, making a cylinder shape. Roll the foil ends in and fold them over. Repeat for all the chicken legs.

    Fill a pan large enough to hold the foil-wrapped chicken halfway with water and bring to a boil. Drop the chicken cylinders in the boiling water and cover with a plate to keep them submerged. Simmer for 25 minutes. After 25 minutes, take the cylinders out and let them cool for about 30 minutes. Unwrap the chicken and discard the foil.

Pour 1 tablespoon of olive oil into an ovenproof sauté pan large enough to hold the chicken and turn the heat to high. Right before the oil begins to smoke, add the chicken skin-down and pop the pan in the oven. Cook until the skin is nicely browned and crispy. Remove from oven, transfer to a plate and keep warm. Discard the oil and reserve the pan.

for the beans:

Bring 2 quarts salted water to a boil. When water is boiling put the fava beans in and **cover**.

Prepare a bowl of ice water large enough to hold the beans.

When the water comes back to a boil, remove the lid and cook until the beans are tender but not mushy. Remove the beans from the boiling water and plunge them into a the ice water. The ice water stops the cooking process immediately, thus keeping the beans beautifully green. As soon as the beans have cooled all the way down, take them out of the water. If left too long, they may waterlog and lose flavor.

to finish the dish:

Heat the reserved pan over medium. Add 1 tablespoon olive oil, the chopped shallot and the mushrooms. Sauté until the mushrooms take on a little color, but be careful the shallot doesn't burn in the process. Turn the heat up to high and add the vinegar and wine. Cook until the liquid reduces by half. Add the chicken stock and continue to cook until reduced to about ¾ cup. Stir in the fava beans and let them warm slightly. Adjust the seasoning

to plate:

Slice the chicken legs into 4 pieces on a bias and fan nicely on a plate. Spoon the mushrooms, fava beans and sauce over the top of the legs.

The reason you want to **cover** the pan is to get the water back to a boil as soon as possible. Nothing will make a green vegetable lose its color more quickly than spending too much time in hot water. When cooking green vegetables, get them in and out of the water as quickly as possible.

However, the idea of covering the pan is bit controversial. Those who say "don't" make the point that covering can cause the vegetables to lose their color. Our contention is that if the pan is covered just long enough to get the water boiling again, there is no harm. We've done it this way for longer than we can remember with no ill effects on the color.

The phone rings and it's a morel hunter telling me he has a basket of morels for me to buy. They are the first ones of the new season. Ah, is this not happiness?

tangerine mousse

1 1/2 teaspoons gelatin
4 whole eggs (Put these into warm water: this makes
    whipping easier and ensures a lighter mixture.)
1/2 cup powdered sugar
1 tablespoon granulated sugar
4 tangerines
2 cups heavy whipping cream
1 empty egg carton

In a bowl that will fit over a 3-quart pot, stir the gelatin into 1/2 cup cold water and let stand.

Prepare an ice bath.

Fill a 3-quart pot halfway with water and bring to a simmer. Using a microplane, take the zest off 2 of the tangerines. Slice all 4 tangerines in half and squeeze the juice into a container. Scoop the pulp out of all 4 shells. Discard the pulp; the 4 shells are going to be used as cups for the mousse.

Lightly whip 1 cup cream to form soft peaks.

Beat the eggs and sugar together in a bowl that will fit on top of the 3-quart pot of water. Gradually add the zest and 1/2 cup of the juice. Place the bowl over the simmering water and continue to beat until the mixture forms a ribbon when the whisk is lifted out — this should take about 6 minutes. It's important to keep the water at a simmer; don't let it boil or you'll have scrambled eggs.

Once the eggs have thickened, remove the bowl from the simmering water and place on top of a bowl of ice. Whisk until the mixture cools. Don't turn the burner off though, as you'll want to use it for the gelatin.

Place the bowl with the gelatin over the simmering water. Leave it there until the gelatin melts, then pour the gelatin into the egg mixture. Stir gently until the mixture begins to set. Working quickly now, take the bowl off the ice and fold in the whipped cream.

Spoon the mousse into a piping bag fitted with a fluted tip and fill the tangerine halves. Place the tangerines halves in the empty egg carton to keep them upright and refrigerate for at least 3 hours.

to serve:

Whip 1 cup of heavy cream with 2 teaspoons of sugar and a dash vanilla extract until stiff. Using a pastry bag fitted with a fluted tip, pipe a dab of whipped cream onto the base of four plates and use it to stabilize the tangerine halves. Pipe the rest of the whipped cream artfully over the top of the mousse.

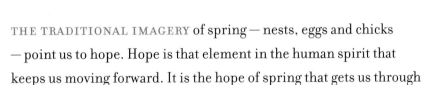

easter

tatsoi and sorrel salad with pickled ramps,
boiled eggs & tarragon

seven hour leg of lamb with fava beans,
peas, savory & goat cheese gnocchi

peaches with cardamom & muscat

THE TRADITIONAL IMAGERY of spring — nests, eggs and chicks
— point us to hope. Hope is that element in the human spirit that
keeps us moving forward. It is the hope of spring that gets us through
winter, the knowledge that winter cannot last forever.

Hope is also the underlying meaning of Easter. And no matter
what our beliefs, we can all take something from the day, and that
something is this: Love can overcome the greatest of obstacles; love
has the power to lift us from the winters of our personal downfalls to
a greater life.

tatsoi and sorrel salad with pickled ramps, boiled eggs & tarragon

We love ramps, or wild leeks, but their season is far too short. Pickling the ramps is our favorite way to stretch the season. In this salad, the ramps are the star of the show.

3 pounds ramps (We'll be pickling more ramps than you'll need for the recipe.)

3 cups rice vinegar

1 tablespoon salt

3 tablespoons sugar

1 lemon rind—only the rind, not the white pithy part

1 teaspoon toasted coriander

1 teaspoon toasted fennel seed

1 teaspoon toasted mustard seed

1 head garlic, cloves separated and peeled

1 arbol chili

4 eggs

3 good handfuls of well-washed tatsoi (Tatsoi is an Asian spinach; regular spinach can be substituted.)

2 handfuls sorrel (There isn't really anything you can substitute here. Sorrel has a truly distinctive flavor.)

1 teaspoon rice vinegar

1 tablespoon olive oil

6-8 sprigs fresh tarragon

Fleur de Sel

In the 1970's the Troigras brothers made **sorrel** famous by making a sauce with it for salmon. That one dish, "Salmon with Sorrel," still stands out as one of the classics of the Nouvelle Cuisine movement. It marked the end of the era of Escoffier and introduced the world to a new way of eating.

If you are good at canning, we suggest putting up a few jars of these leeks in the spring for use when cold December rolls around. Over the summer and autumn, they'll develop a fantastic flavor. They'll also keep nicely for a couple of months in your refrigerator as long as the juice completely covers the leeks at all times.

for the pickled ramps:

Do this a couple of days before you need to use them.

Wash the ramps thoroughly and cut down the tops to just above where the pinkish part starts. You can leave some of the green.

Bring a 2-quart pot of salted water to a boil and prepare a bowl of ice water.

Blanch the leeks for about 30 seconds. What this does is help keep some of the color. As soon as you take them out of the boiling water, plunge them into the ice bath and cool completely. Once the leeks are cooled, put them into the container in which you'll be storing them. Make sure there's enough room for the liquid to completely cover them.

Stir the vinegar, salt, sugar, lemon rind, spices, garlic and 1 cup of water in a pot and bring to a boil. Continue stirring until the sugar and salt dissolve. When the liquid comes to a boil, pour it over the leeks and add the chili. Let the mixture cool before covering and refrigerating.

for the eggs:

Put the **eggs** into a pot large enough to hold them and cover with 1 inch of cold water. The cold water allows the eggs to acclimate as they heat up and keeps them from cracking. Do not put salt in the water as this will cause the eggs to become rubbery.

Heat the pot over high until the water just begins to boil hard. Turn the heat down to a simmer and start your timer. Cook the eggs for **7 minutes**, no more.

Drain the hot water and fill the pot with ice water. Allow the eggs to cool for at least 10 minutes. Don't peel until just before using.

Cooking **eggs** correctly is one of the most difficult culinary processes. Here, we're only going to boil them, but let's boil them right. To get boiled eggs that are easy to peel, you'll need eggs that are a few days old; very fresh eggs don't peel well and you can end up with something that looks like the moon. This is the only time we would ever recommend an egg that isn't as fresh as possible.

The reason eggs get that horrible green color around the yolk is because they are over-cooked. **Seven-minute** eggs give you a yolk that is firm, but juicy — great for salads.

to assemble:

Toss the tatsoi and sorrel together with the rice vinegar, olive oil and a pinch of salt.

Peel the eggs and cut them in half. Place 2 halves on each salad, with 4 or 5 of the pickled ramps. Strip the tarragon off the stem and scatter the leaves over the tops of the salads. (We like smaller items like tarragon in this salad, or bits of parsley, or micro greens, or a sprinkling of chives, or flower petals. It helps create a layered look and gives the salad a more complex appearance. It doesn't just lie there. Little touches like these will give your salads life. Experiment and see what you like.) Finish it off with a touch of Fleur de Sel.

Get into the practice of tasting a leaf of the salad before proceeding so you can adjust. Does it need more vinegar? Olive oil? Too much vinegar or oil? Need a bit more salt?

seven hour leg of lamb with fava beans, peas, savory & goat cheese gnocchi

1 6–8-pound leg of lamb
10 heads garlic, separated and peeled
2 medium onions, cut into medium dice
2 carrots, cut into medium dice
4 stalks celery from the heart, cut into medium dice
1 bottle of good dry white wine
2 cups chicken stock
2 teaspoons toasted fennel seed

1 cup milk
6 tablespoons butter, cut into pieces
1 cup flour
2 eggs
3 sprigs fresh savory, taken off the stem and well chopped
$^1/_2$ cup goat cheese

3 cups fava beans (A good rule of thumb is 1 pound of pods=1 cup
     beans. Take the beans out of the pods and cook until just tender.
     Be sure to shock them in ice water.)

3 cups shell peas (Same rule here as above, but figure 1 pound of
     pods=a little more than 1 cup of peas. Remove the peas from
     their pods and cook until just tender. Shock in ice water.)
olive oil
butter

for the lamb:

Preheat oven to 425 degrees.

Season the leg well with salt and pepper.

Put the vegetables in a roasting pan just large enough to hold the leg. Position the leg on top of the vegetables and put in the oven for about 30 minutes, or until the leg takes on a nice even brown color.

Turn the oven down to 250 degrees.

Remove the pan and add the wine, chicken stock and fennel seeds. Cover the pan with foil and seal. Put the pan back in the oven and let it cook for the next 7 hours. You may want to check the liquid level after a few hours just to make sure it's not getting dry, but if you've sealed the pan well, it should be just fine.

After 7 hours, remove the leg from the pan and allow it to rest. It needs to shed a decent amount of juice, so make sure it resting on something that will catch all of it.

The gnocchi we are
going to make are French
and not Italian, which is
why there's not a potato
in sight. We're partial
to the French-style of
gnocchi partly because
we spent so many years
in French kitchens, but
also because we find
they're lighter in texture
and easier to work with.

Pour the liquid through a strainer and into a pan, making sure you mash as much of the vegetables as you can to extract the juices. Adjust the seasoning and cover to keep warm. Just before serving, put the juice into a serving container with a spoon.

for the gnocchi:

Start by making a *pâté a choux*. (Pâté a choux is the same dough used in éclairs or cream puffs.) In a 1-quart pan, place the milk, butter, 1 cup of water and 1 teaspoon salt. Bring to a boil. Once boiling, add the flour in one shot and mix over medium heat with a wooden spoon until it's a nice, smooth mass. (This mixing over heat ensures that the milk absorbs all the flour.) Remove from the heat and add the eggs, one at a time, stirring thoroughly in between. Once the eggs are mixed in, add the savory and goat cheese.

Prepare a bowl of ice water.

Bring a 4-quart pot of water to a hard simmer. Using a rubber scraper, push the gnocchi mixture to the edge of the pan. With the side of a small spoon, remove a little of the mixture and drop it into the pot of simmering water. Only poach about 6 to 8 gnocchi at a time. The raw gnocchi will sink to the bottom. When they float to the top, let them cook another 30 seconds or so to ensure they're done. Remove with a slotted spoon and place in the ice bath. Once they are cooled in the water, drain them on a towel — the drier the better.

to finish the dish:

There are a couple ways to serve this dish. We could plate the whole shebang in the kitchen and carry it out to the table ... But where's the fun in that?

Sauté the gnocchi in a hot pan over medium high heat in 1 tablespoon olive oil until they're nicely browned. Drain the hot oil. Add the peas and fava beans, along with 2 tablespoons of the cooking liquid from the lamb and a nugget of butter about the size of a walnut. Make sure you swirl the pan so that the butter incorporates into the sauce. Adjust the seasoning.

Take the pan of beans, peas and gnocchi, along with the leg of lamb (on a platter) and some wide-mouthed bowls into the dining room. Don't forget the sauce. Carve the leg in front of your guests. Spoon some of the beans, peas and gnocchi into the bowls. Add enough of the sauce to almost but not quite cover the beans. Arrange the lamb slices on top and dig in.

A FORK IN THE ROAD

RECENTLY I'VE BEGUN to question the place of cooking in my life. What I mean is, where does it fit? What's the purpose?

Paul Tillich, an existential theologian, spoke often of man's "ultimate concern" when referring to God. Faith, he said, is the state of being *ultimately concerned*, and by definition, the concern cannot be something finite. Thus, my cooking, no matter how passionate I am about it, can't be my ultimate concern. So, if cooking can't bring me fulfillment, what can it do? This is the question now before me.

Aristotle taught that by living a virtuous life we can find happiness, and part of living a virtuous life is making the social good of man our highest aim. Put another way, when we place social concerns above individual desires we are living rightly and will find ourselves more fulfilled and thus happier.

Is the greater good of mankind our goal at the restaurant? For now I don't know, but I am going to start off in that direction and see where it leads me. I do know that owning a restaurant for the sake of making money isn't good enough. While we've reached our first anniversary and we have attained the survival goal we set for ourselves, we now need to look ahead with loftier ideals. What are they? At the moment, I haven't a clue. But give us time and I'm sure they'll present themselves. A path for us will be made clear. In the meantime, we're enjoying the adventure.

—E.P.

19 I'm washing a sink full of lettuce. Each leaf has to be handled carefully so as to not bruise it. While picking the various lettuces from their stems or roots, I find myself day dreaming about nothing in particular. Ah, is this not happiness?

peaches with cardamom & muscat

1 bottle Muscat wine
1 vanilla bean, halved with the seeds scraped out
6 pods cardamom, ground — about 1 teaspoon
4 ripe, unblemished peaches

Combine the wine, vanilla bean and cardamom in a pot and bring to a boil. Lower heat to a simmer and cook for 5 minutes. Add the peaches and poach for 15 minutes more. Take the peaches out, turn the heat up to a boil and reduce until about 1 cup of liquid remains. We like this served warm, but it's also delicious cold the next day.

to plate:
Cut the peaches in half, removing the peels and the pits. Arrange two of the peach halves in a bowl and pour on some of the sauce. If you like, a little whipped cream is nice, but so is the simplicity of the plain dish.

It's a beautiful spring evening. The sun is just starting to go down. The restaurant is full. Music is quietly playing in the background. Things are going smoothly in the kitchen and I turn to look out into the dining room and everyone is have such a good time. They are laughing and talking amongst themselves. No one is overly loud but they are lively. A dog on a leash walks by with his owner and he stops to smell the smells coming from the restaurant. Ah, is this not happiness?

THE INCREDIBLE EGG

THE HUMBLE EGG is one of the most important ingredients to be found in the kitchen. Its importance is hailed even by Georges Auguste Escoffier, who said: "Of all the products put to use by the art of cookery, not one is so fruitful of variety, so universally liked, and so complete in itself as the egg. There are very few culinary recipes that do not include eggs, either as a principal constituent or as an ingredient." With this in mind we present the following poem by Clarence Day:

The Egg

Oh who that ever lived and loved
Can look upon an egg unmoved?
The egg it is the source of all.
'Tis everyone's ancestral hall.
The bravest chief that ever fought,
The lowest thief that e'er was caught,
The harlot's lip, the maiden's leg,
They each and all came from an egg.

The rocks that once by ocean's surge
Beheld the first of eggs emerge —
Obscure, defenseless, small and cold —
They little knew what eggs could hold.
The gifts the reverent Magi gave,
Pandora's box, Aladdin's cave,
Wars, loves, and kingdoms, heaven and hell
All lay within that tiny shell.

Oh, join me gentlemen, I beg,
In honoring our friend, the egg.

celebrating heirloom vegetables

salad of butter crunch, flame & paris white lettuces
with tempura of fairy tale eggplant, upland cress,
chrysanthemum flowers & french breakfast radishes

platter of grilled bianca di maggio onions, fresh sardines,
swedish peanut potatoes, lemons & fakir parsley root leaves

moong dahl with early snowball cauliflower
& bloomsdale long standing spinach

charleston "ice cream"

charentais melon soup with homemade yogurt & mint

THOSE OF US WHO were not around before 1951 (the year modern plant breeders introduced hybrids) have grown up on fruits and vegetables that all look exactly alike and have very little taste. Take, for example, an heirloom tomato, and set it beside what our "modern" sensibilities say a tomato should look like. A modern hybrid tomato is perfectly round, firm, shiny and, unfortunately, totally lacking in anything that resembles real flavor. Now, turn to our heirloom: it is often a bulbous mess, certainly not "pretty" and there's not one that looks like the other. But once you taste it, angels begin to sing. The Divine Light shines down upon your cutting board. Epiphany! A word of caution, though: once you start down the path of heirlooms, it quickly becomes an obsession.

This menu is meant to be fiddled with as the heirloom vegetables you find in your market may not be the same ones as listed here. Serve this meal family-style — all the dishes on the table at once.

salad of butter crunch, flame & paris white lettuces with tempura of fairy tale eggplant, upland cress, chrysanthemum flowers & french breakfast radishes

With this salad, we like to set a baby fryer at the table and have everyone tempura their own vegetables. Just toss the salad in the vinaigrette and serve it in a large bowl with the sliced vegetables on the side. In another bowl, serve the tempura batter. You'll need small tongs or a pair of cooking tweezers to dip the vegetables into the batter and a large slotted spoon for retrieving them from the hot oil. You'll also need a plate covered by a clean napkin on which to drain the vegetables when they come out of the oil.

2 Fairy Tale eggplants, thinly sliced lengthwise
    with a vegetable peeler
1 handful upland cress
8 or so chrysanthemum flowers with petals
    removed from stems (Be sure these are organic
    and have not been sprayed with any pesticides.)
8 French breakfast radishes, sliced lengthwise
    with a vegetable peeler

2 egg yolks
1 capful sake (This is optional, but it gives you a perfect
    reason to go out and buy a nice bottle for drinking.)
2 cups ice water
1 $^3/_4$ cups flour

3 handfuls each Butter Crunch, Flame and Paris
    White lettuces
rice vinegar
olive oil
pickled ginger, chopped into small bits (You can
    buy this at any Asian store, but we have included a
    recipe on the next page to make your own, which is
    fun and always tastes better.)
lemon zest

While **tempura** is thought of as Japanese, the idea actually arrived in Japan in the 16th century with European missionaries who were used to making fritters in their home countries. It was the Japanese, however, who lightened up the heavy fritter batter, perfecting it to what we know now as tempura.

for the tempura:

There are a couple of vital keys to making a good **tempura**:

1) Use ice water to make the batter. This makes the batter very cold, and the greater the temperature difference between the oil and the batter, the crisper and lighter the tempura will be. In fact, it's a good idea to keep all your ingredients in the refrigerator until the last minute. The temperature difference also keeps the batter from soaking up too much oil.

543544f

pickled ginger

1 pound young ginger, washed and peeled
salt
1 1/2 cups rice vinegar
1 sugar

Slice the ginger thinly — a mandolin works perfectly for this. Put the sliced ginger into a bowl and add 1 teaspoon salt. Allow to stand for 1 hour.

Take the ginger out of the bowl and dry it on paper towels. Place in a 2-cup container.

Bring the vinegar and sugar to a boil, stirring to dissolve the sugar, then pour it over the ginger. Cover and refrigerate for a couple days to develop its flavor. The ginger will keep in its covered container for a couple months.

2) When mixing the batter, use chopsticks. Unlike a Western fritter batter, you don't want to achieve a perfect smoothness. You want a lumpy, powdery, just barely mixed batter, and to get this, use the worst mixing utensils you have: a pair of chopsticks.

3) Make the batter in small batches and only at the last minute.

4) And this rule goes for all things you will ever fry: do not crowd the frying oil by putting in too many things at a time. Crowding reduces the temperature of the oil and you'll end up *boiling* the vegetables in the oil, which has nothing to do with *frying* them quickly.

Put the egg yolks, sake and ice water in a mixing bowl and stir with a chopstick. Dump the flour all at once into the mixture and stir it together with a few swift strokes. If it seems too thick, add more ice water. (For vegetable tempura, we like a thinner batter because the vegetables are so delicate.)

for the salad:
Toss all of the lettuces in a bowl with a sprinkle of rice vinegar, olive oil and pinch of salt. Mix in the pickled ginger and grate on some lemon zest using a microplane.

to present:
Place the tossed salad greens and the tempura batter in nice bowls beside the baby fryer. The vegetables can be presented on a napkin on a plate. Make sure your guests have the proper utensils at hand.

platter of grilled bianca di maggio onions, fresh sardines, swedish peanut potatoes, lemons & fakir parsley root leaves

12 Swedish Peanut potatoes

6-8 Bianca di Maggio onions
handful chopped fresh herbs

8 or so fresh sardines, have your
    fishmonger scale and gut them

slices of good crusty bread
1 garlic clove

4 lemons
1 Fakir parsley root, leaves only (The root
    can go in the curry dish if you like.)
whole garlic clove, chopped
Kosher salt

for the potatoes:

Put the potatoes in a 4-quart saucepan and cover with 2 inches of cold water. Add a handful of salt. Bring to a boil, then turn down to a soft boil. (If the water boils too hard it has a tendency to tear up the potatoes as they soften.) Cook until a knife can be inserted with some resistance.

    Once the potatoes are cooked, remove from the water and keep warm on a plate. Rub them with some olive oil before grilling.

a word on fresh herbs:

HERE'S A MOTTO we want you to always remember: *No herb is better than dry herb.* If the only herb available is dried, then it's better to forego the use of any herb at all. The dried herbs found in stores around the country are one of the biggest abominations ever to be launched on food. Desiccated store-bought herbs have the power to take the greatest culinary feat and degrade it to mere common grub. We cannot overstate how bad dried herbs are for the taste of your food. One taste and it is immediately obvious that dried herbs were used. Go now to your cupboard and throw those little bottles in the trash. Rid yourself of their heavy yoke.

    However (and there's always a proviso, isn't there?), if you dry your own herbs for use throughout winter, that's a different matter, and by all means use them.

for the onions:

Cut the tops off the onions and reserve. Slice the onions into 3 rounds, like you would for onion rings. Put the onions, without the greens, in a shallow dish. Toss in some of the herbs and a bit of olive oil, along with some salt and pepper. Don't add so much oil that it submerges the onions but enough to make a kind of rub. Rub the oil and herb mixture all over the onions and let set for about 30 minutes. Lightly rub some of the mix onto the greens also.

for the sardines:

Season the sardines with salt and allow to set in the refrigerator for 30 minutes. Lightly brush with some olive oil just before grilling.

for the bread:

Rub each slice with a piece of garlic that has been cut in half lengthwise. Brush each slice lightly with olive oil.

to assemble:

Make a dressing with the herbs, the chopped garlic and olive oil. Invite your guests to squeeze the lemon and drizzle the olive oil-herb mixture onto the grilled pieces on their plates.

Turn the grill on high. When hot, grill the onions, onion greens and sardines. The sardines need to grill 3–4 minutes on each side. The greens onions will cook very quickly. The onions should be marked with a nice criss-cross pattern and then turned over. How long these cook is entirely up to you. Some like them crunchy and some like them tender.

Put the potatoes on the grill and cook until the skin is crispy and shows some color.

Cut the lemons in half and grill on the cut side until somewhat blackened.

Grill the bread until it gets that criss-cross pattern on both sides. When the bread is done, sprinkle with Kosher salt.

Now that everything is grilled, present the food simply on a nice platter, "arranging it artfully," as one classic cookbook puts it. With scissors, snip the parsley root leaves over the whole dish.

It is late afternoon. I brew a pot of my favorite tea and take it down to the dock on the river just behind the restaurant. I watch the ducks diving for food while drinking my tea. Looking up, I see my wife coming down to meet me. Ah, is this not happiness?

QUIETLY OVER TEA

HERE IS A beautiful passage from the book *My Country and My People*, by Lin Yutang:

> *In the years, they have had plenty of time to drink tea and look at life quietly over their teacups, and from the gossip over the teacups they have boiled life down to its essence. They have had plenty of time to discuss … to ponder over their achievements and to review the successive change of the modes of art and life and to see their own in the light of the long past. This became the 'mirror' which reflects human experience for the benefit of the present and future.*

moong dahl with early snowball cauliflower & bloomsdale long-standing spinach

A couple friends of ours, Himanshu and Mukta, who are both from Kashmir, taught us some of the intricacies of Indian cuisine. To get the desired complexity and layering found in good Indian food, it's important to follow the all steps in the recipe. This is because a curry is a gravy in Indian cuisine. It's not a mixture of spices, which is what Americans typically think. The saucy stuff you make here, before you add the lentils and vegetables, is the true Indian curry.

2 cups moong dahl (split yellow lentils)
2 tablespoons clarified butter, see next page
    (You may substitute with soy oil.)
2 tablespoons yellow mustard seeds
2 tablespoons cumin seed, toasted and ground
2 tablespoons tumeric
1 teaspoon asafetida (This is a spice found in East Indian or Mediterranean markets that has a pungent garlic smell.)
2 medium onions, diced very small
2 jalapeños, minced nice and small
1-inch piece of ginger, peeled and minced
2 cloves garlic, minced
1 cup water
2 cups Bloomsdale spinach, stems picked off and chopped into large pieces
2 cups cauliflower, cut into medium-small florets and cooked for 3 minutes in salted water

Wash the lentils 3 times in cold water. Cook the lentils in 2 quarts of water for 25 minutes, or until they are almost soft — you'll want somewhat of a "tooth" when you bite into them. As they cook, skim off the gray foam that comes to the top. Once cooked, drain and set aside.

Mix all of the spices together in a cup.

Heat the clarified butter in a 6-quart heavy-bottomed pot over medium. Add the onions and cook until they're evenly browned. It is very important throughout this entire process to continually scrape up with a wooden spoon the brown stuff that forms on the bottom of the pot. Add the jalapeños, ginger and garlic. Continue to cook — and stir — until these ingredients brown. Reduce the heat to low and add the spice mixture.

Now comes the really important part: a paste will form when you add the spices, but as you cook — and stir and scrape — the paste will eventually break and the oils will separate. This will be obvious when it happens. Slowly stir in 1 cup of water. Done right, the sauce that forms in your pot is genuine curry. Season with salt and pepper.

Stir in the lentils, and when they're warm add the spinach and cauliflower.

to serve:

This is a fine dish to present in a beautiful serving bowl at the table.

clarified butter

THERE IS A DIFFERENCE between clarified butter and drawn butter, even though the two are often used interchangeably. Clarified butter is butter that has had all the milk solids removed; drawn butter is simply melted butter that is served before it separates into its individual components. One pound of solid butter will yield about 1 1/2 cups clarified butter. You can make as little as you need, or clarify a few pounds at a time and divide it into smaller units, freezing until needed.

The method is straightforward. Put the butter in a pan large enough to hold it comfortably with some room to spare at the top. Turn the heat to medium and melt the butter completely. Turn off the heat and leave the butter to set in the pot for 20-30 minutes. After that time, carefully remove the foam that has come to the top.

Pick up the pan up and gently begin to pour the butter into another pot. Don't pour too quickly because you don't want to disturb the milk solids and water that is on the bottom. As you pour, you'll begin to see these solids, and eventually they'll want to run into the pan you are pouring into. When that happens, stop pouring. It's these milk solids that will cause the butter to burn; the water, in turn, causes the butter to spit and pop when it gets hot.

charleston "ice cream"

Charleston "Ice Cream" is the classic way to cook Carolina Gold rice. The recipe comes from the Carolina Gold Rice Foundation, a group whose mission it is to restore and preserve this American rice and other heirloom grains.

3 cups Carolina Gold rice
1 tablespoon butter, cut into pieces

Put the rice into a medium bowl and cover with cold water. Soak for one hour. Drain through a fine mesh colander and rinse.

Heat oven to 200 degrees.

Prepare an ice bath by filling a large bowl halfway with water and ice cubes.

Bring 4 cups of water to a boil in heavy-bottomed, 2-quart saucepan. Add the rice, stirring once. Cover and return to a boil. As soon as the water boils, uncover the pot and reduce the heat. Simmer gently, stirring occasionally, until the rice is just tender, about 5 minutes. Drain through a colander and dump the rice immediately into the ice bath. Stir a bit to chill, then drain.

Spread the rice evenly over a rimmed cookie sheet. Dry in the oven, turning gently from time to time, for 10 minutes. Remove and dot with butter, season with salt and pepper. Return to the oven until the butter has melted and the rice is hot — about 5 more minutes.

to serve:
This also should be spooned into a serving dish and set on the table.

ODDS&ENDS

carolina gold

CAROLINA GOLD is the descendant of a rice that came to the U.S. from Africa in the 1600s. As an immigrant, it was developed under the watchful eye of Thomas Jefferson. Interestingly, he was trying to cultivate an American rice that would have international appeal for export to Europe.

Around 1810, the original Carolina rice was vastly improved upon and renamed Carolina Gold. It is a very versatile grain that can be cooked like a risotto, made into a sticky rice or used in a fluffy pilaf, all depending on how it is treated by the cook.

charentais melon soup with homemade yogurt & mint

This soup is a good study in simplicity. The key is top-quality ingredients. Make sure the melon you use is ripe, the sugar unprocessed, the ice cream of the highest quality and the milk for the yogurt the best you can buy. When ingredients are superb, the outcome will be superb. Auguste Escoffier says it best: "It is just as absurd to exact excellent cooking from a chef whom one provides with defective or scanty goods, as to hope to obtain wine from a bottled decoction of logwood."

$1/2$ cup sugar

1 Charentais melon

2 scoops of good high quality vanilla ice cream (We are lucky enough to have Moomers just a few miles away from the restaurant. *The Today Show* recently called Moomers the best ice cream in the nation. Needless to say, this is our choice.)

juice of 1 lemon

1 quart milk

2 tablespoons existing yogurt with live cultures

mint leaves

for the soup:

Make a simple syrup by boiling $1/2$ cup water with $1/2$ cup sugar. As soon as it comes to a boil, stir to dissolve all the sugar, then turn off the heat and allow the mixture to cool completely.

When the syrup has cooled, cut the melon in half and discard the seeds. Using a spoon, scoop out the flesh and put it into a blender along with the ice cream and a pinch of salt. Blend to purée. Now, taste for sweetness. It's impossible for us to tell you exactly how much of the syrup to put into the purée because every melon has a different sugar level. Adjust the sweetness by adding syrup until you get what you like. After these adjustments, you may need to thin out the purée — use the lemon juice for this. Slowly add the juice until the mixture has the consistency of a soup.

for the yogurt:

Make the yogurt the day before you need it.

Allow the yogurt culture to come to room temperature.

Heat the milk until it almost boils. What you are looking for is the formation of small bubbles around the edge of the pan. If you have a thermometer, watch for 180-185 degrees F. Don't heat too fast: the process should take about 15 minutes.

Let the milk cool until it gets below 120 degrees. Stir often so as to get a more accurate reading because you don't want to let it cool below 90 degrees. With the milk at the right temperature, mix in the yogurt culture and transfer to a clean container. Cover with plastic and let it stand for anywhere between 8 and 15 hours in a warm spot — the best place is in the oven with a pilot light. The temperature should be between 105 – 115 degrees.

When the yogurt is fairly firm, move it to the refrigerator. The thin yellow liquid that will form is called the whey. It can be poured off or stirred back into the yogurt.

To assemble:
Ladle the soup into bowls. Spoon a dollop of yogurt on top and sprinkle with some chopped mint.

It's a chilly, drizzling Saturday morning. I'm up early as it's opening day for the farmers market, and with much anticipation I make my way over. Walking around to the various stalls I'm able to catch up with farmers I haven't seen since last year. We talk about our families, the state of business, health, what they have planted and what I should expect as the summer progresses. Though there isn't much for sale yet, ah, is this not happiness?

a fancy late spring lunch

salad of tender greens, crispy capers,
pancetta & almonds

soft shell crab, broccoli rabe & chipotle sandwiches

apricots poached with ginger & lime

LATE SPRING announces the arrival of soft shell crabs. From May
to July the culinary world is blessed with these wonderful creatures.
A soft shell crab is simply a blue crab that has outgrown its shell. There
is a four-day period of time between the shedding of the old shell and
the hardening of the new one; this is when the crab needs to be eaten.
Cooking soft shell crabs is not for the queasy, as we shall see as we go
along, but the end result is truly worth the effort.

WE HAD A YOUNGSTER working for us a few years ago who had
not yet discovered the joy of cooking. She always wanted us to give
her exact measurements. How many tablespoons of this? How
many cups of that? What we were trying to teach her was to *feel* the
food. We wanted her to learn to *listen* to the dish. To *understand*
when the food says, "All right, that's enough."

You see, we can't cook without heart. A recipe is not something
to be followed with scientific detachment. If we cook like that the
dish will never have character. The book of Genesis tells us, "The
LORD God formed man of the dust of the ground, and breathed
into his nostrils the breath of life; and man became a living soul."
The cook must breath soul into his dishes in order for them to
live. The breath of life comes not from the cookbook, but from
the cook.

It's 8:00 in the morning. I don't expect anyone in
for the next couple of hours. There is a favorite radio
program playing quietly in the background. It's just
me in the kitchen with a short prep list, so I don't
have to hurry much. Taking my steel in my hand I
put a good edge on my knife and slowly get to work.
Ah, is this not happiness?

23

salad of tender greens, crispy capers, pancetta & almonds

This salad is meant to be a side course for the main event, which is why we've kept it simple.

$1/4$ cup olive oil

3 tablespoons capers, let them drain on some paper towels until dry

2 slices pancetta about $1/4$-inch thick, strips cut into $1/4$-inch-wide pieces and cooked until brown and crispy

$1/2$ cup slivered almonds, roasted until you smell them (We have found that when you need to toast spices or roast nuts, the best way to judge when they are roasted/toasted enough is by smell. A chef we know says it perfectly, "The nose knows.")

5 or 6 handfuls of tender, young greens (Greens in late spring are at their most delicious, and your best bet for finding them will be at a farmers market. Look for greens that are small and young, and find a nice mixture of these if possible.)

rice vinegar

Vegetables from farmers markets are often dirty, but dirt on your produce is a good thing. For example, you can get a sense of how fresh the produce is by the moistness of the dirt. Also, soil on the produce means it hasn't been washed yet, and produce really shouldn't be washed until you're ready to use it. Wash produce too early, and it loses its freshness.

Be careful here: whenever you work with oil and **high heat** you need to be diligent. Make sure you have a slotted spoon ready because once the capers are in the oil, they will fry quickly and you'll want to get them out even more quickly.

To make the crispy capers, heat the olive oil over **high heat**.

When the oil is good and hot, carefully add all the capers at once. They will splatter, so don't panic. As they cook, you'll notice that the bubbling slows down. Once it slows down to the point where it isn't bubbling much at all, pull them out with the spoon. This will take a minute or so. Drain them on a paper towel.

Put the salad greens into a bowl and drizzle on enough olive oil to moisten the lettuce. Add about 1 tablespoon rice vinegar and a pinch of salt. Toss with the pancetta, almonds and capers. Plate.

Jen and I often part ways when it comes to the subject of assembling salads. She prefers to toss all the ingredients together, then plate. I like to toss the greens in the oil and vinegar and sprinkle the other ingredients on top. Both ways are just fine and it really comes down to personal preference. Play with it and decide for yourself.   —E.P.

soft shell crab, broccoli rabe & chipotle sandwiches

4 soft shell crabs (It is of utmost importance to assure these
are alive, lively and plump.)

**$^1/_2$ pound broccoli rabe (aka rapini) cut into
$^1/_2$-inch pieces**

1 clove garlic, cut very thin (Think of this as your chance
to slice the garlic á la "Goodfellas." Remember the
dinner scene in which the narrator is telling the story of
how Paulie used a razor to cut the garlic? It gives us the
chance to get in touch with our inner mobster.)

1 cup chipotle mayonnaise (see facing page)

**1 loaf ciabatta bread, cut into 4-inch squares and then
sliced in half so you have a top and bottom**

1 cup flour

Grill the ciabatta — it brings out the flavor of the bread.

Sauté the garlic in 1 tablespoon olive oil in a large (large enough
to hold the 4 crabs) fry pan over medium heat for 2 minutes. Add the
broccoli rabe, season with salt and cook for 5 more minutes. Remove the
broccoli rabe and reserve on a plate. Discard the oil — we'll use the pan
again in a minute to cook the crabs.

Put the flour into a bowl and season with salt and pepper.

Clean the crabs (see below).

cleaning the soft shell crabs:

Here comes the hard part. To clean the live crabs there are 3 things you have to do:

1) Using scissors, cut off the face.

2) On the bottom of the crab, there is a tail-like flap called "the apron"—cut this off.

3) Lift up the sides of the shell and you will see some feather like things—cut these out.

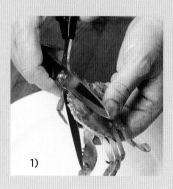

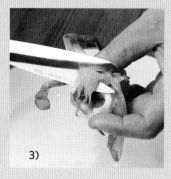

1)   2)   3)

jeremy's chipotle mayonnaise

1 egg
1 1/2 cups olive oil
2 tablespoon rice wine vinegar
1 lime, just the juice and zest
1 shallot, peeled
2 cloves garlic, peeled
2 ounces chipotle chilis in adobo sauce
    (This can be found in most Mexican
    grocery stores.)
3 tablespoons fresh cilantro

Place the egg, vinegar, lime juice and zest, shallot, garlic, pepper and cilantro along with 1 teaspoon salt and 1 teaspoon pepper into a food processor. Cover and blend for 45 seconds. Remove the cover and slowly begin adding the olive oil in a thin stream. You'll notice the sauce thickening up. If it gets too thick and you still have some oil left, add a little water to thin it down and continue adding the rest of the oil.

What will happen if the sauce gets too thick is that it will break. I remember breaking a mayonnaise during my apprenticeship and going to Chef Andre to let him know. He looked at me, and with his thick French accent said, "So fix it!" Now, I wasn't sure how to boil water at this point and he wanted me to "Fix it!" I stood there, looking like dork, having no idea what to do next. "I, ah, don't know how to fix it," I admitted. With all the compassion a French chef can muster for his lowly apprentice (this is, of course, tongue in cheek), he told me to get a bowl and a whisk. After retrieving these items for him, he put about a tablespoon, or perhaps a little more, cold water into the mixing bowl and very slowly started to add the broken mayonnaise. This restarted the emulsion I'd botched the first time around. "There," he said to me, "that's how you fix it!"   —E.P.

Dredge the crabs in the flour.

Add another tablespoon of olive oil and reheat the fry pan over medium-high. When it's almost smoking, add the crabs, top side of the shell first. Sauté for about 3 minutes. Turn the crabs over and sauté for 3 more minutes. Be careful, as soft shell crabs often have the last laugh in that they like to pop and splatter hot oil everywhere. Not much fun, but an obstacle that must be surmounted to enjoy the little beauties.

to assemble:
Spread the chipotle mayonnaise on both sides of 2 pieces of bread. Put the broccoli rabe on the bread first and top with the crab. Place the other piece of bread on top.

apricots poached with ginger & lime

$1/2$ cup sugar
$1/2$ cup Riesling
piece of ginger about the size of a wine cork,
    cut in half lengthwise, then each half cut
    into 6 pieces
1 vanilla bean, split in half with the beans
    scraped out
12 firm, ripe apricots
zest of 2 limes

Mix the sugar, wine and $1/2$ cup water in a pot and bring to a boil. Stir well until the sugar dissolves. Add the ginger and the vanilla. Simmer for 5 minutes. Add the apricots and simmer 2 more minutes. Remove from the heat, add the zest and allow to cool.

When the mixture has cooled, remove the apricots. Cut them in half and discard the pits. Put the apricots back into the sauce.

to serve:
Divide the apricots into bowls and spoon over some of the sauce.

Suddenly, and out of nowhere, an idea pops into my head for a new dish. The day continues but the idea remains and will noodle around until I act on it. Gathering all the necessary ingredients together, I start the process of bringing the new idea to life. On the first attempt, the new dish is exactly what I had envisioned. We all try it and agree it is excellent. I decide not to put it on the menu. Ah, is this not happiness?

SO I GET A PHONE CALL the other day.

"Thank you for calling The Cooks' House," I say.

"Are you 100% organic? I only eat organic," comes the reply.

"Excuse me?"

"Organic. I *only* [emphasis hers] eat in places that can serve me organic foods, and it is very difficult to find those places in Traverse City."

"Um, we serve locally grown products ..."

"Yes," she interrupts. "But are *those* [emphasis hers] products organic?"

"I can't guarantee it." I was becoming irritated by *this* [emphasis mine] interrogation. "You see," I continued, "we place our emphasis on supporting the local farmers. I do know they all are very conscientious about their growing practices and most of them practice organic or natural methods, meaning they don't use traditional pesticides."

"*So* you *don't know* how the farmers grow the food you sell?"

"Not to the extent that I can guarantee what is organic and what is not. Like I said, we are trying to support the local farmer, and the ones we buy from practice very ecologically safe growing methods."

"I guess I can't eat in your restaurant because you don't know if what you serve is organic or not."

"No, I guess you can't."

I hung up.

Organic or not organic? This is the question. I don't fault those who try to use only organic products. I agree that it's a great idea, but it's not always feasible for the restaurant or the farmer. We have the privilege of knowing almost all of the farmers and producers of everything we buy, and have talked to more than a few of them about their growing practices. There is a common response from those farmers who are not *one hundred percent certified organic*: it's too damn expensive a process to get the certification from the regulating governmental agency. To support these people, we've stopped worrying about organic and have placed our focus on finding those individuals who practice sound methods. Our concern and focus is on the *local*, not the *organic*. We find it much more ecologically sound to buy a naturally grown apple from our local area than an organic one shipped in from Chile. Feel free to snub your nose, but make sure that glass you use is made using fair trade practices.

—E.P.

I had a guest ask me about how to poach an egg. I wasn't busy and invited her to come into the kitchen to show her. After discovering it isn't all that difficult, she smiled. Ah, isn't that happiness?

25

summer

Summer in the world;
floating on the waves
of the lake.

—BASHO

in honor of bernard loiseau

eggplant caviar with zucchini sauce

frog legs with garlic purée & parsley sauce

blackberries with ricotta, granola & wild honey

luncheon, family-style

radishes three ways

smoked whitefish with onion purée
& pea shoots

purslane with baby beets,
braised beet greens & bacon

roasted halibut with spinach &
cucumber-saffron vinaigrette

strawberries in red wine with
hibiscus tea ice cream

a midsummer's night picnic

grilled figs wrapped in pancetta

walker's pesto passion

orzo, radicchio, chick pea & herb salad

rhubarb tarts

saint euphrosynos

updated waldorf salad

braised lamb shanks with apples, turnips & lentils

classic tart tatin

in honor of
bernard loiseau

eggplant caviar with zucchini sauce

frog legs with garlic purée & parsley sauce

blackberries with ricotta, granola & wild honey

BERNARD LOISEAU (January 13, 1951–February 24, 2003) has had more influence on my cooking than any other chef. I have always felt a kinship with him, even though I never had a chance to work for him, or even meet him. Loiseau's approach to cooking was as pure as one could ask. Above all else, he believed that the flavor of the ingredient should never be interfered with. He believed this so much that early on he refused to use anything but water when he needed a liquid for a dish. Only a true master could pull off serving food so simply prepared. We offer the following menu in Chef Loiseau's memory. The dishes are not directly from his recipes, but they were born of his ideas. —E.P.

eggplant caviar with zucchini sauce

2 medium eggplants (Too large and they begin
        to lose flavor.)
olive oil

1/2 onion, sliced any way
2 medium zucchinis (Not too big for the same
        reason as the eggplant. A rule of thumb: The
        bigger the vegetable, the less the flavor.)
1 clove garlic
lemon
rice vinegar
olive oil
4 sprigs parsley or chervil,
        or 4 large basil leaves

for the caviar:

Cut the eggplants in half and score the flesh rather deeply with a paring
knife in a crosshatch fashion. Opening the slits, sprinkle the flesh inside
lightly with salt. Rest the eggplant cut-sides down in a colander for 30
minutes. (The salt causes the eggplants to release some juice, and with it,
some of the bitterness.)

While the eggplants are draining, preheat oven to 350 degrees.

After 30 minutes, place the eggplants cut-side down on a baking
sheet covered with oiled parchment paper. (Eggplants have a tendency to
react to aluminum negatively, so we always put paper under them before
roasting.) Oil the skin-side of the eggplants to keep them from drying out
and make it easier to scoop out the flesh.

Roast for 1 hour. Allow the eggplants to cool enough that you can handle
them. Scoop the flesh onto a cutting board and discard the skin. Chop the
eggplant finely.

In a 10-inch frying pan, pour 1 tablespoon olive oil and turn the heat
to high. As soon as the oil begins to smoke, add the eggplant. Using a
whisk, quickly stir for about 1 minute, then pour into a mixing bowl.
Continue mixing until you get an even purée. Adjust the seasoning. Add 1
tablespoon more olive oil and 2 teaspoons vinegar. Taste again and adjust.
You want the eggplant flavor up-front; in the background should be hints
of the olive oil and vinegar. Don't let the oil and vinegar compete with the
eggplant. Set aside.

for the zucchini sauce:

Remove the stems and chop the zucchini in a medium dice — keep the skins on. Put the dice into a blender and add enough water to barely cover. Squeeze in half a lemon's worth of juice and add 1 teaspoon salt. Crush the garlic clove (skin removed) with the side of your knife and put that into the blender also. Blend on high speed until very smooth. Taste and adjust the seasoning.

to plate:

Ideally, use a set of rings or a mold that is open on both ends. The size of the mold should be 2 ½ inches wide and 1 ½ inches high, but if your dimensions are slightly off, don't fret; just use what you have and do your best. The ability to improvise is an important trait in all good chefs.

Put the ring mold in the middle of a plate. Scoop the eggplant caviar into the mold until it reaches about 1 ½ inches in thickness. Lightly tap the plate on the tabletop to set the caviar. Spoon enough zucchini sauce around the mold to cover the plate. Carefully remove the mold and garnish with the herbs.

My son is at the restaurant, hanging out. He is not doing anything in particular except looking up points of interest on the Internet. Just when I'm at my busiest in the kitchen he wants to show me something, and although I don't really have time, because he is with me I make time. He shows me something trivial. We look at each other knowingly. Ah, is this not happiness?

frog legs with garlic purée & parsley sauce

This is a Loiseau classic. It isn't his recipe, but I think he would have approved. For example, look at how many ingredients there are. I count eight, and that includes the salt and pepper. The reason Loiseau could serve a dish like this in a Michelin three-star restaurant is because he used only the best ingredients and combined those with the skill and technique of a master. These are the two most important rules anyone can learn about cooking. Follow these rules and you will produce world-class food — no fancy tricks needed, no clever gimmicks necessary.

—E.P.

10 heads whole garlic, separated but in their skins

2 or 3 bunches flat leaf parsley, leaves removed from the stems (It is very important to the texture of the sauce that there be no large stems. Large stems equal stringy sauce.)

24 pairs (48 single) frog legs
3 cups olive oil
3 to 4 cups flour

for the garlic:

Put the garlic in a pot of water and bring to a boil. When the water boils, pour it out and start again. Do this 3 times. What you're doing is getting rid of the strong garlicky taste. After the third boil, pour out the water and peel the garlic. Push the peeled garlic through a steel mesh strainer into a bowl. Season with salt, cover and keep warm. Wash the strainer because you're going to need it for the next step.

for the sauce:

Ready a bowl of ice water.

Bring a 4-quart pot of salted water to a boil. Add the parsley, covering the pot, and cook for 2 minutes. Pour the parsley and water into a strainer, then plunge the strainer into the bowl of ice water. Mix to ensure the leaves get cold as quickly as possible — this will keep them a nice bright green. Once cooled, put the parsley into a blender with enough of the ice water (minus the ice) to equal about ¾ of the mass of the parsley. Blend until a smooth purée is obtained. Be careful not to blend too long because the friction from the spinning blades will make heat and ruin the color.

for the frog legs:

If the frog legs came in pairs, chop them in half so all the legs are single. Cut off the 2 two muscles. Fold the leg meat down over itself to get what looks like an upside-down lollipop. The French name for this technique is *jambon*, which is the word for "ham" because it looks like a little bone in ham.

Season the trimmed legs with salt and pepper and dredge lightly in the flour.

Put a 3-quart pot on a medium flame and add the olive oil. Fry the legs in 3 batches, allowing the oil to reheat after each batch. Fry until the legs are golden brown. Drain on a paper towel. You may find it necessary to reheat the legs quickly before serving. If so, use a sheet pan in a 500-degree oven.

to plate:

Put a dollop of the garlic purée in the middle of each large plate. Heat the parsley sauce in a small pan over medium (it may be necessary to add a bit of water to thin it out). Adjust the seasoning and spoon the sauce around the purée. Arrange 12 frog legs around the purée and sauce. Your guests should use their fingers and you can set out finger bowls of warm water and lemon slices.

27

It's Saturday morning, my absolute favorite time of any week. I'm walking the farmers market, looking at the produce. As I move around the grounds, one of my favorite farmers pulls out from underneath his table a dozen guinea hen eggs he gathered just that morning and asks if I'm interested. Without hesitation, I buy them and then spend the rest of my time moving from vendor to vendor looking for ideas with which I can pair the eggs for that night's service. By the end of my time, I have a basket full of new items and a new dish in my head featuring guinea hen eggs. Ah, is this not happiness?

TODAY BEFORE COMING TO WORK I was reading an article by Thomas
McNamee in an old *Saveur* magazine. In it, McNamee was recounting
an internship he took through an organization called L'Ecole des Chefs
that helps get passionate amateur cooks into some of the top kitchens
in France and elsewhere in the world. He was lucky enough to spend
his time in a couple of Paris' best restaurants. I'd like to share the last
paragraph of the article because I think it does such a wonderful job of
summing up my feelings towards those who cook at the highest levels.

—E.P.

*It comes down to this: I used to deem Tuscan cooking the best.
"A thing on a plate" was my aphorism for it; let the ingredients
speak. Now I know that I was confusing good cooking with artistry
… In my internship, I didn't learn how to make puff pastry or master
Six Secrets of the Great French Chefs. I learned that bringing to
cooking the rigor and passion and limitless labor of the artist can
transform food into an experience as deep and memorable as that of
more enduring works. I learned that doing it demands a life spent
doing it. Great art is always expensive, always rare, always oblivious
to the injustices that make it possible. The fact that these astonishing
meals disappear into one's experience of them, in fact, gives them a
unique power rooted in mortality: The coucou de Malines die and are
made glorious for our pleasure, and in doing so they disappear. Like
them, we shine, if we're lucky, and then we die.*

blackberries with ricotta, granola & wild honey

1 tablespoon sugar
1 teaspoon vanilla extract
8 ounces ricotta
1 cup granola
1 1/2 pints blackberries
wild honey

> We have no qualms with **vanilla extract** and think it has its place in every kitchen. Some chefs turn up their noses, saying that it's cheating, but we disagree and find extract to be useful.

procedure and plating:

Mix the sugar and vanilla thoroughly into the cheese. Spoon 1/4 of the cheese mixture into the middle of a plate. Sprinkle some granola and then the blackberries over the top. Gently warm the honey (warm, not hot) and drizzle it over the berries and around the plate.

Later that day I get a call from the farmer who sold me the aforementioned guinea hen eggs, wanting reservations for dinner. I am able to serve him the dish I created with his eggs. Ah, is this not happiness?

JUMPING SHIP

WE HAVE A COOK HERE who is leaving the kitchen confines and joining the waitstaff. I can't believe it. For the most part this amounts to treason. What makes it all the worse is the fact that he is doing it for the money. For the money! Sure, it's true that waiters always make more than the cooks — they always have. But for a cook to decide that money is more important than the kitchen is an outrage.

Cooks have always harbored a distrust and dislike of waiters. Waiters are of a completely different breed. They come into work looking sharp. Their hands are manicured. Their hair is combed just so. They never sweat. Their clothes are always perfectly clean. They work half the hours of cooks but make more money. Shall I go on? OK, I shall. Waiters have to be pampered. They don't know what a hard day's work is. I mean, really, what is their job, anyway? Take an order and make sure the customer gets what he wants? Whoop-de-do.

Meanwhile, look at the cooks. We are almost always tired. Our hands and arms are beat up with scars from burns and cuts. We sweat like stuffed pigs. We never smell good when we go home at night. We make dick in the money department. The customer usually doesn't even know we exist. Tips? Please ... On a rare occasion we may get *one*. We take abuse from the chef on a regular basis. We do not have a social or family life. I mean, it takes *real love* to cook because the conditions are not always the best. *We do it because we love it.*

There is a brotherhood amongst cooks. Waiters? They are a rabid pack of wolves who will eat each other at a moment's notice for a chance at a bigger tip.

As you can now see, I don't take it lightly when a cook decides to jump ship and go over to the other side. It just shows me that that person doesn't have what it takes to survive in the kitchen.

So, here's my message to the new waiter: Good luck, buddy.

—E.P.

luncheon, family-style

radishes three ways

smoked whitefish with onion purée & pea shoots

purslane with baby beets,
braised beet greens & bacon

roasted halibut with
spinach & cucumber-saffron vinaigrette

strawberries in red wine with hibiscus tea ice cream

THIS MENU IS for a warm evening when you should be
outside under the beautiful summer sky, passing dishes
back and forth, laughing and drinking wine — not cooped up
in a hot kitchen trying to time everything just right.

radishes three ways

$^1/_2$ cup each, washed and with greens removed:
    French Breakfast radish, Icicle radish,
    Red radish
2 cups rice vinegar
2 tablespoons plus 1 teaspoon sugar
1 lemon
1 cup chicken stock
sea salt

for the icicle radishes:
Prepare 2 days ahead of time.
Place the radishes in a medium-sized bowl and set aside.

In a pot, bring the rice vinegar, 1 cup water, 2 tablespoons sugar and 1 tablespoon salt to a boil. While this is cooking, remove the rind from the lemon with a vegetable peeler. (Try not to remove too much of the white pithy part because it's extremely bitter.) When the mixture boils, remove it from the heat and pour over the radishes. Add the lemon rind. Allow the radishes to pickle for 2 days in a cool, dark place.

for the french breakfast radishes:
Place the radishes in a pot just large enough to hold them and cover with 1 cup chicken stock. Add 1 teaspoon of sugar, a nugget of butter the size of an olive and a pinch of salt. Bring to a boil and cook until the liquid is reduced and the butter and stock form a sauce.

It is possible to **reduce** a stock too far. You'll know if this happens because your nice sauce will break. You can bring it back together by adding a little water and stirring. Of course, too much water and your sauce will get thin and you'll have to reduce. This can become a vicious circle so be careful the first time.

for the red radishes:
Brace yourself for some technical cooking: Chop off a little bit of the bottom of each radish to make a base. They should be able to stand upright.

Cover the bottom of a plate with some good sea salt.

Here comes the hard part: Stand the radishes flat-side down in the salt. How did you do? Hope the stress didn't get to you. Actually, we absolutely love radishes like this; it's one of our favorite before-dinner snacks. It just goes to show if you have a great tasting product, there isn't much you need to do to it.

to serve:
Each variety of radish should be served in its own dish. The French Breakfast radishes should be served warm.

smoked whitefish with onion purée & pea shoots

2 yellow onions
2 tablespoons butter plus 1 tablespoon chilled butter
1 cup milk

1 smoked whitefish (An equal amount of smoked trout or
    haddock will also work, but don't use salmon because the
    flavor's too strong.)
1 egg yolk
1 orange, the zest in one bowl, the juice in another
1 lemon, the zest in the same bowl with the orange zest,
    but only $1/2$ the lemon juice added to the orange juice
$1/2$ teaspoon fresh grated ginger
2 teaspoons mustard (We use Brownwood Farms' "Famous
    Kream Mustard" at the restaurant. It's made just a few miles
    north of us and is one of the best anywhere.)
$1/2$ cup salad oil
2 tablespoons chopped fresh chives
$1/4$ pound pea shoots

Low heat is very important when cooking onions. Too-high heat will turn the onions bitter and brown. The low heat ensures that the onions stay very sweet and white.

for the purée:

Chop the onions into medium pieces and purée in a food processor.

Melt 2 tablespoons of the butter in a 2-quart saucepan over low heat. Stir in the onion and season with salt. Cover the pan and let cook slowly for 25 minutes, stirring every 5 minutes.

After 25 minutes, add the milk and turn the heat to medium. Cook for another 5 minutes. Transfer the onions to a blender and add the chilled butter. Blend to make a very smooth purée. Adjust the seasoning, transfer to a bowl and chill.

The trick to any emulsion is adding the oil **slowly** at first. If you add it too fast, then there won't be enough volume built up to hold the oil and the sauce will break.

What do you do if you break the mayonnaise? You'll have to start over — no, not the whole thing, just the emulsion. Put a little water, about 2 teaspoons, in another bowl, and slowly — key word here is *slowly* — whisk in the broken sauce. Once the emulsion has formed, you can start adding the oil again.

for the whitefish:

Pick the meat off the whitefish bones, making sure to get rid of all those pesky pin bones, and place in a bowl.

Make a mayonnaise by whisking together the egg yolk, zest, juice, ginger, mustard and a pinch of salt in a medium bowl. Start adding the oil while whisking, slowly at first. When the sauce forms, you can add the oil faster.

Continue adding the oil until it's all incorporated. If the sauce is thin, add a little extra oil. Reserve about 1 tablespoon of the mayonnaise. Mix the remaining mayonnaise and the chives into the smoked whitefish. Be careful to mix gently so as not to break up the fish too much.

to plate:

Heap the whitefish in a nice serving bowl. Toss the pea shoots with the reserved sauce and arrange them on top of the whitefish. Serve the chilled onion purée in another bowl.

purslane with baby beets, braised beet greens & bacon

Purslane is a fantastic leafy green, but when it's on the menu, we always get the question, "Is this what grows in my yard that I try to kill every summer?" Yes it is. *Don't kill it, eat it!*

This particular dish can be made into a salad by not sautéing the purslane, rather tossing it uncooked in some vinegar and oil.

$^1/_2$ pound baby beets with greens still attached (When we say baby, we mean really, really, tiny. What you want are beets that are about $^1/_4$-inch in diameter, length is not important. If you can only get larger ones, then you'll need to cook them longer than this recipe calls for.)
1 cup chicken stock
butter
$^1/_4$ pound purslane, washed and cut into 3-inch pieces with the large stemmy parts discarded
8 slices bacon, cut into $^1/_4$-inch pieces
$^1/_4$ onion, diced small
1 teaspoon mustard
olive oil

Place the beets — greens and all — in a pan large enough to hold them. Add the chicken stock, an olive-sized nugget of butter and a pinch of salt. Bring to a boil, then reduce the heat and cook until a nice sauce forms and the beets are tender. If you need to, add a little more water and cook longer. Put aside (in the pan) and keep warm.

In a fry pan large enough to hold the purslane, add the bacon, onion and 2 teaspoons olive oil. Cook over medium heat until the bacon browns. Add the purslane and sauté for about a minute and a half. Check the seasoning — there is a good chance you will not need salt. We always wait until the very end to season this dish as purslane can have a naturally salty flavor. Stir in the mustard, mixing well.

to plate:
Spoon the purslane into a serving dish and top with the beets and greens. Pour any remaining sauce from the beets over the top.

QUESTION AUTHORITY

LATELY I'VE BEEN questioning everything I do in the kitchen, revamping the reasons and the ways I've been doing things for the last 20 years. Questioning habits and beliefs opens the mind to progress. If a cook never questions why he or she does something, then that cook never grows, never gets better. Yesterday, I scrapped the crêpe recipe I was taught during my apprenticeship because I've never really liked it. I came up with a new one and it's better. I've changed my knife stroke when I cut chives. I've started messing around with how I poach eggs. I've noticed that I am more mindful of temperature when I sauté. Do I really need everything I put into my chicken stock? Is it necessary to cook the fish/chicken/meat so long? Does the dish really need to be cooked at all, or can I just leave it alone?

Questioning the basics is exciting. It feels like getting back to the essentials of cooking, the simplicity of it. And this re-examination of one aspect of my life has led to the questioning of everything about myself as I have long made the same mistakes over and over out of habit. Now, I'm making a concerted effort to change those things that are useless and sloppy. It's hard and it can only end when I end.

—E.P.

roasted halibut with spinach & cucumber-saffron vinaigrette

We love vinaigrettes for fish. Too often, fish is served with heavy, over-the-top sauces that mask its delicate taste. Vinaigrettes are a great alternative to a heavy sauce.

$^1/_4$ cup rice vinegar
1 teaspoon saffron
$^1/_2$ cucumber, peeled, cut in half lengthwise with the
  seeds scooped out, then diced into a fine dice
1 shallot, minced
1 smallish clove garlic, minced
$^3/_4$ cup fruity olive oil
$^1/_8$ cup chopped chervil or parsley (We really prefer
  chervil for this dish because it's so much more delicate
  and it adds a slight lemony hint to the vinaigrette.)

4 to 6 8-ounce pieces of halibut, seasoned all over
  with salt and placed meat-side down on a
  napkin to dry
olive oil
butter
$^1/_4$ pound fresh spinach, stems picked off
$^1/_4$ onion, chopped small

for the vinaigrette:

Put the rice vinegar and saffron in a small pan and warm gently. Do not let it boil. What you're doing is using heat to draw out the flavor of the saffron. When the mixture's warm, pour it into a bowl and steep for 15 minutes.

You always want to season the vinegar with the **salt** before adding oil because salt doesn't dissolve very well in oil. By adding it before the oil, you can be sure the salt has dissolved.

  Add the cucumbers, shallots, garlic, 1 teaspoon salt and a dash of pepper. Whisk in the olive oil.

  Just before serving, add the chervil. Chervil is a very delicate herb and the vinegar will eat it up if it is added too soon.

for the fish:

Preheat oven to 400 degrees.

In an ovenproof frying pan large enough to hold the fish, pour 1 tablespoon or a bit more olive oil. Turn the heat to just under high. Before the oil starts to smoke, add the fish, meat-side down. Cook until it's nice and brown on the bottom.

Carefully turn the fish over and add 1 tablespoon butter to the bottom of the pan. Slide the pan into the oven and cook for 8 minutes. Baste at about the 4-minute mark. Baste again when you remove the fish from the oven.

While the halibut is in the oven, cook the spinach.

In a large pot, place the chopped onion and 1 tablespoon olive oil and turn the heat to medium. Sauté until the onion is translucent. Add the spinach, seasoning with salt and pepper. Using tongs, turn the spinach until it loses its volume. Switch to a spoon and sauté for 1 additional minute.

to serve:

Spoon the spinach onto a serving platter. Arrange the fish on top. Serve the vinaigrette in a bowl on the side.

It can be very disheartening when all that **spinach** cooks down to nothingness. On the other hand, it's given me great pleasure to watch more than one youngster cook his first large batch. After spending a lifetime picking off those damn stems, the look of dejection is worth the price of admission. —E.P.

a word on saffron:

SAFFRON used to be rare and precious, but it can now be found in almost any grocery store. Look for Spanish or Iranian saffron, and try to use "threads" rather than "powdered." The threads (actually the stigmas of *Crocus sativus*) are a much better tasting product.

It takes anywhere between 70,000 to 200,000 fresh, hand-picked flowers to produce one pound of dried saffron, which makes it the world's most expensive spice. Fortunately, it doesn't take much to get a strong flavor. Yes, it is possible to have too much of a good thing: use saffron sparingly. Remember, the key to great cooking is subtlety.

strawberries in red wine
with hibiscus tea ice cream

8 egg yolks
$^2/_3$ cup sugar
2 cups milk
1 vanilla bean, split in half or 1 teaspoon vanilla extract
1 cup heavy whipping cream, whipped to form soft peaks
5 teaspoons hibiscus tea, loose leaf preferable (If there are only tea bags available, then use 4 bags.)

20 or so medium strawberries, cut in half (If, by some chance, the gods of cooking smile upon you and grant you the grace of a couple baskets of wild strawberries, by all means jump at the opportunity, and use those instead.)
2 cups red Zinfandel
$^1/_2$ cup honey
1 teaspoon lemon zest
1 teaspoon orange zest

for the ice cream:
Prepare this the day before you plan to serve.
Whisk the egg yolks and sugar together in a bowl until a ribbon forms when you draw up the whisk.

Pour the milk into a 1-quart pan and scrape in the vanilla bean seeds and add the pod. Bring to a boil and add the tea. Remove from the heat and allow to steep for 10 minutes.

Bring a pot of water — large enough to hold the bowl with the egg yolks — to a simmer.

After 10 minutes, taste the milk. You want a rather strong flavor because the addition of the whipped cream and the freezing will diminish the flavor. Steep longer for more flavor. Discard the pod.

Pour $^1/_4$ cup of the hot milk into the egg yolk mix and stir. Still stirring, slowly add the remaining hot milk. Place the bowl over the simmering water and cook, stirring with a wooden spoon or a rubber scraper, until it thickens enough to coat the back of a spoon. Remove from the heat and cool completely. Fold in the whipped cream and freeze.

A dried vanilla bean **pod** added to a bowl of sugar, makes vanilla-sugar. Try it.

If you were to leave the custard **unfrozen**, you'd have a dessert sauce called *crème anglaise*.

for the strawberries in red wine:
Wash the berries well and cut them in half. Mix the wine, honey and zests in a pot and bring to a boil. Stir until the honey melts. Remove from the heat and allow to cool until just warm. Pour over the strawberries and marinate, unrefrigerated, for 1 hour.

to serve:
Divide the strawberries evenly among the dishes and pour enough wine on top to not quite cover. Drop a healthy scoop of the ice cream in the middle. Dig in.

a midsummer's night picnic

grilled figs wrapped in pancetta

walker's pesto passion

orzo, radicchio, chick pea & herb salad

rhubarb tarts

SUMMER makes it easy for us cooks. Most of the time, all we have to do is pick and plate.

grilled figs wrapped in pancetta

Few fruits or vegetables can compete with our love of figs. There are so many ways to prepare and to pair them. The following recipe is a favorite, although we also like them in a salad with arugula, olive oil, lemon juice and parsley.

12 fresh figs
12 parsley sprigs
6 thin slices pancetta, cut in half
olive oil
1 lemon, cut into 8 wedges, each wedge cut
    in half crosswise
Fleur de Sel

Pancetta is an Italian-style bacon made out of pork belly, salt-cured with spices, then dried for about 3 months. Pancetta is not usually smoked. It can be bought from most specialty markets, although it's becoming more and more common all the time. We wouldn't be surprised if you find it in your local grocery store.

Cut each fig in half from top to bottom. Place a parsley sprig on the cut sides, then wrap each half in a piece of the pancetta.

If you have a grill, turn it on high. Without a grill, use a cast iron skillet on medium-high heat.

Brush the wrapped figs with a little olive oil — not too much or the oil will drip down into the grill and flame up, producing an oily, black soot on the figs. Not very tasty. Same goes if you're using a cast iron skillet, but for different reasons. Too much oil in the skillet will make greasy, fried figs. Again, not very tasty. So, lightly brush the wrapped figs with the oil and place cut-side down on the grill, or in the pan, and cook until the bacon is crisp, about 2 minutes.

to serve:
Squeeze some lemon and sprinkle a little salt on the figs before popping them in your mouth.

LAST SUPPER

· ·

WHILE BROWSING the cookbook section in our local bookstore, we ran into
something called My Last Supper: 50 Great Chefs and Their Final Meals, by
Melanie Dunea. We thought it was an irresistible exercise, this planning of a
final, perfect meal. The questions below are taken directly from the book. You
can find our answers at **thecookshouse.typepad.com**. We invite you to post your
own thoughts about a "Last Supper" there as well.

What would be your last meal on earth?

What would be the setting for the meal?

What would you drink with your meal?

Would there be music?

Who would be your dining companions?

Who would prepare the meal?

A slice of bread with butter and honey. Ah, is this
not happiness?

· ·

walker's pesto passion

Walker is a good friend of ours and she adores pesto. During the summer months we put this sandwich named after her on the lunch menu. It makes a great picnic selection because it's simple, refreshing and always delicious.

3 tomatoes, ripe but firm
olive oil

1 cup basil
1 tablespoon pine nuts
1 garlic clove
olive oil

1 loaf ciabatta bread, or other rustic variety
3 balls fresh mozzarella
olive oil
1 handful arugula, tossed in a little olive oil
　　and a pinch of salt

We always use **parchment** or wax paper when baking on sheet pans to keep food from taking on a metallic taste and to prevent the food and the pan from discoloring. The parchment also makes the pans a lot easier to clean.

for the tomatoes:

Preheat oven to 350 degrees.

Put some **parchment paper** or wax paper on a sheet pan.

Slice the tomatoes about $\frac{1}{2}$ inch thick — you'll probably get 4 or 5 slices from each.

Place the sliced tomatoes on the pan and sprinkle with salt and pepper. Drizzle some olive oil on top. Bake in the oven for 30 minutes or until the tomatoes begin to color. (What you're doing is drying the tomato out. By getting rid of excess water, you're concentrating the flavor, making it taste more *tomatoey.*)

for the pesto:

Purists make **pesto** with a mortar and pestle. If you're like us, you'll use a food processor. Put the basil minus stems, the garlic, pine nuts and just enough oil to make a paste into the hopper. Blend on high until you get a leafy paste. (Don't go too long or the heat of the blades will discolor the basil.)

Jen and I have a running disagreement when it comes to **pesto**. How it's served on any given day at the restaurant depends on who gets there first. Jen roasts the garlic and the pine nuts because she doesn't like the taste of the raw garlic in the pesto and prefers the roasted flavor of the pine nuts. I, on the other hand, don't like to roast the pine nuts or the garlic because I think the nuts get too strong and I don't like

the color it lends the pesto. Also, I *do* like the taste of raw garlic and I think it gives a nice hit to the spread. Choice is up to you. Do you side with Jen or with me? —E.P.

P.S. If you do insist on roasting the garlic and the pine nuts, be sure you let them cool before making the pesto as the heat will cause the basil to turn black.

to assemble the sandwiches:

Slice the ciabatta bread into 4-inch squares, then cut those squares in half so you have the top and bottom of a sandwich.

Cut the mozzarella balls into ½-inch slices.

Brush some olive oil on the bread halves and grill them until they're toasty and golden brown. On the bottom slice of the sandwich, place 3 slices of mozzarella, then 3 or 4 slices of the tomato. Add the arugula. On the top slice of bread, spread a good amount of pesto. Press the 2 halves together, and voilá.

At this point, Jen and I have another disagreement: whether or not to slice the sandwich in half. She thinks it's easier to eat sliced, while I think it makes less mess unsliced. If these were the hardest choices in life, I'd have it made.   —E.P.

30 It's been a rather long week and I am particularly tired. After a busy lunch service I sit down to write out the dinner prep list. Though the sun has been shining most of the day, it begins to cloud over and a light rain shower ensues. The door is open making it possible to smell the fresh air. For some reason, the tea I'm drinking tastes better than normal. Even though I'm tired, a feeling of wellness overcomes me and I sit back and enjoy a peaceful moment. Ah, is this not happiness?

orzo, radicchio, chickpea & herb salad

3/4 cup dried chick peas
6 cloves garlic, peeled
2 sprigs thyme
1 bay leaf (Keep your eyes peeled for fresh bay leaf. It's out there.)

1 1/2 cups orzo

1/2 head radicchio
2 good handfuls mixed herbs (Choose from basil, marjoram,
       chives, fennel tops, chervil, etc. Take the leaves off and throw
       away the stems. Don't chop.)
olive oil
zest from 1 lemon
2 teaspoons honey
1/2 shallot, finely chopped
olive oil
rice vinegar

Soaking dried beans ensures a quicker cooking time and also helps the beans cook more evenly.

It's a myth that cooking beans in **salted** water makes them tough.

for the chickpeas:
Soak the chickpeas overnight in cold water. They must soak at least 12 hours, but 24 hours is best.

Preheat oven to 250 degrees.

Drain the beans and add them, along with the garlic, thyme and bay leaf to a heavy pot with a lid. Fill the pot with water so that there is 4 times more water than beans. Add 3 or 4 teaspoons salt. Bring the beans to a boil, cover and place the pot in the oven. Cook for the next 2 hours, checking after the first hour to ensure there's enough liquid. When the beans are tender, they're ready.

for the orzo:
Cook the orzo just like you would any other pasta. Make sure you salt the water.

for the radicchio:
Turn the grill to high. Cut the half-radicchio in half again and brush it lightly with olive oil. Grill each side for 2 minutes, then let it cool. Once cooled, cut it into slices that are 2 inches long and 1/4 inch wide. Reserve.

for the vinaigrette:
Stir the honey, shallot, about 2 tablespoons vinegar, 1 teaspoon salt and some pepper in a bowl. Stir well to dissolve the salt. Whisk in the oil.

to assemble:
Put all the various parts of this salad in a big bowl and mix in the vinaigrette. Adjust the seasoning.

rhubarb tarts

This is one of our most popular desserts. We almost had a riot last year when we took it off the menu because rhubarb went out of season.

1 ½ cups sugar
½ cup rum
2 pounds rhubarb (If the rhubarb is thick, then you'll need to peel it. Use a paring knife for this and take the skin off in long strips starting at the root-end of the stalk.)
½ lemon

a little more than ¾ -stick butter, cut into small pieces and softened
1 ⅔ cups flour
¼ teaspoon salt
4 egg yolks
½ teaspoon vanilla extract
1 whole egg
1 tablespoon milk
coarse sugar

for the filling:

Make a simple syrup by combining 1 cup of sugar with ⅓ cup of water and the rum in a 3-quart pan. Bring to a boil over high heat. Stir until the sugar dissolves.

Chop the rhubarb into ½-inch pieces and stir into the simple syrup. Bring to a boil and reduce the heat to a steady simmer. Cook for about 20 minutes, then squeeze in the lemon juice. You want the filling to thicken, but if it cooks too much it will be difficult to spoon into the crusts. Pour the filling into a bowl and allow it to cool completely.

for the crust:

This is a French dough called *pâte sucrée*.

Make a pile of the flour on a countertop or other flat surface. Hollow out a well in the center and add the butter, egg yolks, vanilla and salt. Mix with your fingers. Form into a ball, using a spatula or pastry scraper to get all the bits of dough.

We're going to quote Escoffier for the kneading procedure: "When the paste is mixed, roll it into a mass; put it on the board then press it away from you, little by little, between the board and the palm of the hand. For the paste to be perfectly smooth, it ought to be treated twice in this way." If the dough is sticky, add a bit more flour. After the second kneading, seal the dough in plastic wrap and let it rest for at least 1 hour in a cool place. Don't put the dough in the refrigerator as the butter will harden and you won't be able to roll it out.

After the dough has rested, divide it into 4 pieces.

It's very important that you don't work in a hot kitchen when making pastry. Too much heat softens the butter, making the dough difficult to work with. This is also why you want to let pastry dough rest in a cool place.

When Jen and I were at Andre's in Las Vegas, we developed a theory about **plate sizes** and men. The theory goes like this: Ask any guy to give you, say, a 5-inch plate. He will almost always give you a 7-inch plate. Ask him to give you a 7-inch plate and he'll give you a 9-inch plate. We tested this theory over and over again with all the male cooks or waiters who worked with us and proved it more times than not. Anytime a new guy would start at the restaurant, we'd immediately ask him to give us a certain size plate and he would usually give us the next size larger. Read into that what you like — I know we have — but give it a try for yourself and see if we're not right.   —E.P.

to assemble and cook the tarts:

Preheat oven to 350 degrees.

Roll each piece of dough to the size of a 7-inch plate; it doesn't have to be perfectly round.

Spread ½ cup of the cooled rhubarb mixture into the middle of each tart round, leaving a 1-inch border round the edge. Fold the border up and over onto the filling to make a pie casing.

Make an egg wash by mixing the whole egg and a tablespoon of milk together in a small bowl. Brush the egg wash onto the tart crust and sprinkle generously with coarse sugar.

Put the tarts on a sheet pan with wax paper and cook in the oven for 20 minutes, or until the tart is nice and golden brown. Let cool.

There is a feast planned and a spit-roasted whole lamb is the centerpiece. Because the lamb will take so long to cook, the day has to start early and everybody is tired. There is a struggle getting the lamb wired on the spit so it turns evenly, but along with this struggle there is laughter at the difficulties. Then begins a heated debate about how to arrange the coals for proper roasting. But after the lamb is on the spit and the coals have been arranged, we sit down for the long, patient roasting. A couple of hours into it, another friend arrives with a loaf of bread and some bottles of wine. We sit there drinking wine and sopping up the juices off the roasting lamb with the bread and telling stories. Suddenly I realize that finishing the lamb in no longer the point. Ah, is this not happiness?

saint euphrosynos

updated waldorf salad

braised lamb shanks with apples, turnips & lentils

classic tart tatin

APPLES HAVE ALWAYS been associated with Saint Euphrosynus, and the following menu features apples in each dish. Saint Euphrosynus' feast day is September 11, which for us cooks has made that day one of both sadness and celebration. Perhaps this dinner can serve those dual purposes: in remembrance of those who lost their lives on that fateful day in 2001, and for the humble cook's saint.

"You lived righteously in great humility, in labors of asceticism and in honesty of soul O righteous Euphrosynos. Hence, by a mystical vision, you demonstrated most wondrously the heavenly joy which you found. Make us worthy to be partakers thereof by your intercessions."

TROPARIAN TO SAINT EUPHROSYNOS

SAINT EUPHROSYNUS, PATRON SAINT OF COOKS

EUPHROSYNUS WAS a monk in a 9th-century monastery. Because he was uneducated, he was relegated to serve in the kitchen. Often demeaned and abused by the senior monks, Euphrosynus remained humble and obedient, and continued to cook for them. He became the patron saint of cooks because he found his salvation while stirring boiling pots in his kitchen.

Now, don't worry, this isn't a religious education class. What I want to focus on is the existential aspect of the story. We cooks find our "salvation" in the heat of the kitchen. For Paul Tillich, an existentialist theologian, salvation is defined as fulfilling the ultimate meaning of life. While cooking is not the ultimate meaning of life for me, it is the vehicle which allows me to search, and at times find out, what life is about. This is the way I approach my life in the kitchen. It is in the kitchen I find meaning and truth.

Like our ancestor Saint Euphrosynus, cooks of today are often still looked down upon by those for whom we cook. I'm not talking about the chefs who have attained celebrity status, for they are a tiny minority. I'm referring to those of us who cook in anonymity. I have always told young cooks to cook for themselves, because if they cook for fame, or acknowledgment, or to keep the boss happy, or, or, or …, they will not find fulfillment. They will not find, if I may, salvation.

—E.P.

updated waldorf salad

2 cups apple cider
1 tablespoon rice vinegar
1 teaspoon mustard
1 cup salad oil

1 egg, separated
2 teaspoons sugar
2 cups walnuts
2 crisp apples (Honey Crisp is good for this, or Gala
    or Granny Smith.)
$1/2$ cup celery leaves, taken from the hearts
    (Use the hearts with the lentils below.)
olive oil
mixed greens
zest of 1 orange

for the dressing:

Reduce the apple cider in a small saucepan to $1/2$ cup. Allow to cool.

Pour the cider into a small mixing bowl with the vinegar, egg yolk, mustard and a dash of salt. Whisk well. Slowly — and we mean slowly — pour in the oil, whisking all the while. As the emulsion begins to form, you can speed it up, just not so fast that you break the dressing. (See page 180 for details about emulsions.)

for the salad:

Preheat oven to 375 degrees.

Whisk the egg white and sugar in a mixing bowl until somewhat fluffy. Add the walnuts and mix well. Pour the mixture into a strainer and let stand for 5 minutes. This will drain off any excess egg white.

Spray a cookie sheet with pan spray and spread the walnuts on it, seasoning with pepper — but no salt. (If you salt now the walnuts will not crisp up.) Place the sheet in the oven and bake for 5-8 minutes. Pull them out when they're nicely browned and allow to cool. Once cooled, you can break them up and season with salt.

Julienne the apples and place them into a bowl with the celery leaves. Drizzle with olive oil and season ever-so-lightly with salt. Mix well.

to plate:

Toss the mixed greens with some of the dressing and a pinch of salt. Divide on 4 plates. Grate orange zest on top using a microplane. Sprinkle some of the walnuts on top of the lettuce and top with the apple-celery mixture.

a word on classic dishes:

I LOVE THE CLASSICS and have no qualms about using them as they are or as a springboard to create something new. My cooking background is French, so I tend to gravitate toward that "classic" end of the spectrum, but every cuisine around the world has its own canon.

I have it heard it said that a painter must first learn to paint "classically" before reaching out to a more modern approach. In my opinion, the same goes for the cook, whether he or she comes from an Asian background or French, Mexican or Indian. If a cook wants to progress to the point of creating new dishes, then he must first learn the classic dishes of his tradition.

I always advise a new cook to pick a cuisine he likes and learn the dishes that make up its foundation. Without a solid foundation of the chosen cuisine, the cook cannot progress in his skills because he'll be lacking a focal point. Progress without focus is very difficult. With a solid foundation in place, branching out with new ideas becomes much simpler.

—E.P.

braised lamb shanks with apples, turnips & lentils

4 lamb shanks
2 tablespoons garam masala (An East Indian spice mixture.)
1 onion, rough chopped
5 star anise
fennel seed
$^1/_2$ bottle good white wine

$^1/_8$ cup carrot, cut into small dice
$^1/_8$ cup celery, cut into small dice
$^1/_4$ cup onion, cut into small dice
1 teaspoon madras curry powder
1 $^1/_2$ cups French green lentils (These are, without a
    doubt, the best lentils around. They hold their shape
    even when cooked. Plus, they taste amazing and
    have a great mouth-feel.)
4 $^1/_2$ cups chicken stock

1 large turnip
sprig of thyme
1 apple (This should be a good cooking apple like
    Jonathan or Braeburn.)
1 tablespoon sugar

fresh cilantro

Always use a **wine** for cooking that you would also drink out of a glass. The quality of the wine will affect the finished product. A cheap wine will give a cheap flavor, while a better wine will bring complexity to the finished product. We saw a t-shirt once that made us laugh. It said, "I love to cook with wine. Sometimes I even put it the food."

Celery hearts, with their milder flavor, blend better with most foods. You have to be careful when working with celery because of its tendency to be too forward.

for the lamb shanks:

Season the shanks with salt, pepper and the garam masala. In a pan just large enough to hold the shanks, place the onion, star anise and a few pinches of fennel seed. Place the lamb shanks on top of the onions, pour on the wine, then cover with plastic wrap and seal with foil. (The purpose of the plastic is to keep the foil from touching the food; the foil keeps the wrap from melting.)

We suggest using a crockpot for this. Turn it to low, go off to work and come home to some tender shanks. If you don't have a crockpot, preheat the oven to 300 degrees. Cook the shanks in the oven for 4 – 5 hours. You'll know they're done when the meat lifts easily off the bone. When the shanks are cooked, remove them from the pot and strain the juice into a saucepan.

for the lentils:

In a 4-quart saucepan, heat 1 tablespoon of olive oil over medium-low. Toss in the carrots, celery and onion. Add the curry powder and a dash of salt. Cover and cook until the onions are translucent and soft. Add the lentils and 3 ½ cups of the stock and bring to a boil. Reduce to a medium simmer and cook until the lentils are tender, about 30 minutes. Adjust the seasoning.

for the apples and turnips:

Preheat the oven to 350 degrees.

Take a large square of foil and put it into a small, ovenproof pan. Place the turnip in the middle. Add a sprig of thyme and sprinkle of olive oil. Form a package out of the foil and cook in the oven for 1 hour. Let cool. When the turnip is cool enough to handle, cut it into a medium dice. We like to leave the peel on as it has great flavor.

Cut the apple into a medium dice, again keeping the skin on. Put a walnut-sized nugget of butter into a 9-inch fry pan and turn heat to high. In a bowl, toss the apples with the sugar. When the butter in the pan is hot, add the apple-sugar mix. Cook, tossing the apples occasionally until they turn light golden brown. Toss in the turnips, cooking for another minute. Add 1 cup of chicken stock and bring to a boil. Boil for 45 seconds. Adjust the seasoning.

To plate:

Into 4 larger-sized bowls, divide the lentils evenly. If you like, you can take the shanks off the bone. This makes eating much easier for the guests, and the guests' comfort is always the most important. Place one shank on top of the lentils and top with a scoop of the apples and turnips. Pour some of the broth over the shanks and sprinkle with the cilantro.

a word on seasoning:

FIRST OF ALL, when a cookbook or chef asks you to "adjust the seasoning," 99 times out of 100 they're referring to the salt and pepper levels. To "adjust the seasoning" then, means to add more salt, and sometimes pepper, if needed.

Seasoning is one of the hardest lessons to learn in cooking. It takes thousands of practice dishes. Here's a rule of thumb for salt: When you salt, what you're looking for is a *lack of flatness*. Oftentimes cooks want to "sharpen up" a dish, and they think that will happen by adding more salt. The problem with this thinking is that "sharpness" and "correct seasoning" are usually different problems needing different solutions. By tasting for a lack of flatness, you're keeping your palate focused on the right problem. Once the salt has been adjusted, then you can turn to matters of "sharpness," or whatever the dish may be lacking.

Here's the trick: Before you salt a dish, taste it by slurping it with as much air mixed in as possible. This lets you taste it *as it is*. Once you think you've reached that point of "lack of flatness," stop and let your palate rest. After 5 or 6 tastes, the palate grows numb and can fool you.

classic tart tatin

10 tablespoons butter
$1/4$ cup sugar
1 vanilla bean or 1 teaspoon vanilla extract
2 pounds or so cooking apples (Gala, Cortland,
      or Rome Beauty), peeled, halved and cored
1 sheet puff pastry, thawed out to $1/2$-inch larger
      in diameter than your pan

$1/2$ cup whipped cream

Preheat the oven to 425 degrees.

Butter the sides and bottom of a high-sided, 8-inch oven-safe sauté pan. Pour the sugar into the pan, adding 2 tablespoons water and the vanilla. Turn the heat up to medium-high and cook until the sugar is melted and beginning to turn golden. Turn off the heat. (At this point, be careful working with the sugar. If it gets on your hands or arms it's like napalm.)

With the pan still on the burner — but the heat off — carefully set the halved apples side-by-side, straight up and down all around the pan and into the middle. If you have extra, put them aside. As the tart cooks, you can use them to fill holes.

ODDS&ENDS

tart tatin:

LIKE SO MANY THINGS we love, tart tatin is a product of serendipity. Tradition has it that around 1888-ish, Stephanie Tatin created the dish. Stephanie and her sister owned the Hotel Tatin in France's Loire Valley, and each one was in charge of different aspects of running the business. Stephanie was in charge of the kitchen, her specialty being a caramelized apple tart. One day during the rush, Stephanie, who apparently wasn't the sharpest knife in the kit, put the tart into the oven upside down. When she realized her mistake, it was too late and she decided to serve it anyway. So there it went to the table, still warm and upside down. The customers loved it! Tart Tatin is one of perfect case studies on how little is needed to make something taste so good.

P.S. Andre Rochat, my mentor and teacher for many years, used to tell me that my hell will have me buried up to my chin in warm tart tatin without a fork to be found and no way to eat it. Thanks, Andre.

—E.P.

Set the pan into the oven and cook for about 15 minutes. Keep an eye on it for a couple reasons:

1) If you have extra apple halves, you can put them into the pan as room becomes available

2) You want the bottom of the apples to become a nice golden brown. To check this, you'll have to take the pan out of the oven and, using a pair of tongs, carefully lift one of the halves out to look at it. Don't worry if the apples don't brown evenly.

When the apples are a nice golden brown, take the tart out of the oven and slide the puff dough on top, allowing the edges to droop over the sides.

Put the tart back in the oven and cook another 15 minutes, or until the pastry is good and brown. (It's important that the pastry is nicely browned, because under-cooked puff pastry is chewy and not very tasty.) Take it out of the oven and allow to cool for about 7-8 minutes.

Now comes the tricky part. Find a 9- or 10-inch plate and set it, upside down, on top of the tart. Pick up the pan with one hand and put the other hand, palm down, on top of the plate. In one swift motion flip the pan over. Now you have the plate on the bottom and the pan on top. Do not, we repeat, do not hesitate when flipping. Hesitation may lead to *tart tatin au brouillé* (scrambled tart tatin).

You may need to bang the bottom of the pan with the handle of a knife to loosen any sticking apples. Good. Now sit down and breathe. Have a drink of water (or something stronger if the mood strikes you). Congratulations! Flipping your first tart tatin is a daunting but extremely satisfying accomplishment.

to serve:
Whip the cream with 1 teaspoon of sugar and serve on top of the tart. Eat this warm, always.

It's a Sunday afternoon and the restaurant is closed, but for some reason my family and I are here. The sun is shining and there is a cool breeze blowing and I have the door open. There aren't many people on the street but occasionally someone pops their head in to see if we're open. I'm not doing much of anything but fiddling around. The family tells me they're hungry and I make a simple lunch for us. We sit at one of the tables eating and talking about nothing. Ah, is this not happiness?

32

THERE ARE THREE stages to any taste: beginning, middle and end. The beginning is whatever you get when you put something in your mouth. Seasoning — whether it needs more salt or, God forbid, it's over-salted — is what you should notice during the middle part. The end of the taste is either missed or ignored by 98% of the cooks out there, counting pros and amateurs alike. The end of the taste is that part that separates good food from great food; from food you forget quickly to food you remember long after dinner is over.

Finishing a dish requires that you make the taste linger, in much the same way a great wine's taste lingers. It is one of the hardest things to do in cooking and it requires the use of some tricks, including lemon zest or an acid, like vinegar. We've also used Godiva Chocolate liqueur to stretch out the flavor of a Chestnut and Foie Gras Soup. Ginger and horseradish will sometimes work. Each dish requires something slightly different. Chef Grey Kuntz has a fantastic cookbook that covers this area of cooking much better than we can in this short space. The book's called *The Elements of Taste*. Go out and get yourself a copy.

33 Being a cook. Ah, is this not happiness?

index

Anchovies, 126
Andre's French Restaurant, 11, 196
Apples
    with duck, 71
    with lamb, 202
    in salad, 21, 200
    tart tatin, 204
Apricots, 161
Aristotle, 139
Artichokes
    soup, 43
    trimming, 43
Arugula, 36

Bacon
    in biscuits, 99
    in salad, 182
    in soup, 55
Balance, 21
Bayless, Chef Rick, 23
Beans
    in cassoulet, 108
    cooking, 192
    fava, 129, 137
    white, soup, 32

Beef
    in cassoulet, 108
    short ribs, 84, 108
    tenderloin, 36
    veal cheeks, 112
Beer
    in braise, 23
    Bell's Lager of the Lakes, 23
Beets
    braised, 182
    greens, 44, 182
    in salad, 44
Bible
    Genesis, 156
    John 12:24-26, 53
Biscuits, 99
Blackberries, 175
Blending, 119
Boar, 110
Bok Choy, 46
The Book of Tea, Okakura, 48, 111
Braise, 58
Bread Sauce, 58
The Breath of Life, 156
Brioche, 76
Broccoli Rabe, 158
Burdock Root, 46
Butter
    clarified, 149
    and Fernand Point, 104

Cabbage, 112
Cactus, 21
Cake
    chocolate, 88
    Greek Honey-Walnut, 122
    mousse, 89
    trifle, 88
Camus, Albert, 83
Capers, 157
Caramel, 28, 29
Carolina Gold Rice Foundation, 152
Cassoulet, 108
Cauliflower, 149
Caviar
    eggplant, 168
    Great Lakes, 80
Celery Hearts, 202
de Champlain, Samuel, 78
Chard, 98
Cheese
    blue, 39
    cake, 39
    cheddar, 99
    Comte, 94
    cream, 39
    goat, 137
    Grassfield, 94
    Kase, Roth, 94
    mascarpone, 88
    Parmesan, 34
    Upland, 94
Cherries
    in braise, 23
    juice, 100
Chestnuts, 67
Chick Peas, 192
Chicken
    braise, 23
    cooking temperatures, 96
    stuffed, 129
    processing and raising, 96, 97
    resting, 97
    roast, 96
    stock, 113
    stuffing, 96
    trussing, 96

Chocolate
    braise, 23
    cake, 88
    Godiva Chocolate liqueur, 88
    Mexican, 23
    mousse, 89
    trifle, 88
Choosing Seeds, 114
Chorizo, 21
Christmas
    cactus flower, 68
    celebrating, 66, 72
Classic Cookery
    and cassoulet, 108
    cuisine, 58
    in French Onion Soup, 95
    and pig trotters, 104
    sauces, 78
    as a springboard, 201
Clarified Butter, 150
Clove, 63
Cooking
    with oil, 157
    and purpose, 139
Cooking, Peterson, 99
Cooks, 25, 156, 177
Cornmeal, 120
Court-bullion, 32
Craft, 40
Crème Anglaise, 186
Crock Pots
    for braised lamb shanks, 202
    for braised short ribs, 84
Croutons, 95
A Crown of Thorns for the Plum
    Pudding, 72
Curry, 149

Dashi, 46

Daube, 104

Day, Clarence, 141

Desserts

    Apricots Poached with Ginger
        and Lime, 161

    Blackberries with Ricotta, Granola
        and Wild Honey, 175

    Blue Cheese Cheesecake with
        Pear Compote, 39

    Caramel Flan, 28

    Charentais Melon Soup with
        Homemade Yogurt and
        Mint, 153

    Classic Tart Tatin, 204

    Dried Fruit Cobbler, 100

Greek Walnut-Honey Cake with
    Earl Grey Ice Cream, 122

Peaches with Cardamom and
    Muscat, 140

Rhubarb Tarts, 195

Stewed Plums with Vanilla and
    Muscat, 49

Strawberries in Red Wine with
    Hibiscus Tea Ice Cream, 186

Tangerine Mousse, 132

Traditional Plum Pudding, 73

Warm Indian Creamed Rice
    with Pomegranates and
    Pistachios, 63

White and Dark Chocolate
    Trifle, 88

The Devil in the Kitchen, 83
Dishing the Dish, 90
Duck
confit, 108
roast, 71
Dumplings, 124
Dunea, Melanie, 189

Easter, 133
Eating Art, 174
L'Ecole des Chefs, 174
Eggplant
caviar, 168
Fairy Tale, 143
Eggs
boiling, 135
and Day, 141
and Escoffier, 141
seven minute, 135
The Elements of Taste, Kuntz, 206
Emulsions, 180
Entrées
Braised Lamb Shanks with Apples,
Turnips and Lentils, 202
Braised Veal Cheeks with Cabbage,
Raisins and Potatoes, 112
Cassoulet, 108
Chicken Legs Stuffed with
Sausage, 129
Chicken Thighs Braised in
Chocolate, Chili Peppers,
Dried Cherries & Stewed
Tomatoes, 23
Daube of Venison, 104
Frog Legs with Garlic Purée and
Parsley Sauce, 172
Grilled Bianca di Maggio Onions,
Fresh Sardines, Swedish Peanut
Potatoes, Lemons and Fakir
Parsley Root Leaves, 145
Roast Chicken, 96
Roast Duck Stuffed with Onions
and Juniper Berries, 71
Roasted Halibut with Spinach
and Cucumber-Saffron
Vinaigrette, 184

Roast Pheasant with Watercress
and Cauliflower Salad and Bread
Sauce, 58
Roast Quail on Polenta with
Dried Plums, 120
Sautéed Walleye with Great
Lakes Caviar and Champagne
Sauce, 80
Seven Hour Leg of Lamb, 137
Short Ribs Braised in Red Wine and
Star Anise, 84
Soft Shell Crab, Broccoli Rabe and
Chipotle Sandwiches, 158
Trout Poached in Miso Broth with
Baby Bok Choy and Burdock
Root, 46
Walker's Pesto Passion, 190
Whole Roasted Beef
Tenderloin with Wilted Arugula
and Crushed Fingerling
Potatoes, 36
Wild Boar Ragout with Root
Vegetables, Curly Kale and
Cavatappi Pasta, 110
Escoffier, Georges Auguste, 56, 101,
141, 153, 195
Existentials, 162

Fakir Parsley Root, 145
Farmers Markets, 157
Figs, 188
Fish & Seafood
bonito flakes, 46
cookery, 80
halibut, 184
trout, 46
walleye, 80
sardines, 145
smoked whitefish, 180
soft shell crab, 155, 158
vinaigrette for, 184
Flan, 28
Fond
definition of, 97
formation of, 121

Foie Gras
    in brioche, 76
    au Torchon, 77
A Fork in the Road, 139
Frog Legs, 172
Frontera Grill, 23
Frying, 144

Garlic
    confit, 119
    purée, 172
    varieties of, 32
Garnishing, 121
Ginger
    pickled, 143, 144
Gnocchi, 137
Granola, 175
Le Guide Culinaire, Escoffier, 101

Hannah Montana, 63
Hazelnuts, 78
Heirloom Vegetables, 142
Herbs, 145
Hoffman, Hans, 56
Horseradish
    dumplings, 124
    preparing, 124, 125

Ice Cream
    Earl Grey, 122
    Hibiscus Tea, 186
    Moomers, 153

Jerusalem Artichokes
    origin of, 78
    purée, 119
Jesus, 53
Jumping Ship, 177
Juniper Berries, 71

Kale
    braised, 98
    in ragout, 110
    in soup, 32
Keats, John, 33
Kelp, 46
Kuntz, Grey, 206

Lamb
    braised, 202
    Seven Hour Leg, 137
Last and First Men, Stapleton, 69
Last Supper, 189
Leeks (see also Ramps)
    baby, 84
    pickled, 134
Lemons
    cooking with, 43
Lentils
    in braise, 202
    moong dahl, 149
Life Is Already Too Complicated, 62
Lin, Yutang, 147
The List of Five, 51
Local Food, 162
Loiseau, Bernard, 167, 172

Mâche, 68
Mayonnaise
    Jeremy's Chipotle, 159
    recipe, 180
McNamee, Thomas, 174
Melon, 153
Miso, 46
Mushrooms
    porcini, 129
    in ragout, 34
    wild, 34
Mussels
    soup, 32
Mustard
    Brownwood Farm's Famous
      Kream, 180
    greens, 98
My Country and My People, Lin, 147
*My Last Supper: 50 Great Chefs and Their
    Final Meals*, Dunea, 189

New Year's Eve, 75
No Death, No Fear, Thich, 53
Nouvelle Cuisine, 56, 134

Nuts
    almonds, 157
    oils, 68
    roasting, 157
    walnuts
        in cake, 122
        in salad, 200
        in soup, 43

Of Bulls and Ballerinas, 25
Okakura, Kakuzo 48, 111
Onions
    Bianca di Maggio, 145
    cooking, 94, 180
    soup, 94
    purée, 180

Organic, 162
Oysters
    stew, 67

Pans
    cleaning, 28, 190
    cooking with, 121
    covering, 130
Parchment & Wax Paper, 190
Parsley
    Fakir, 145
    sauce, 172
Pasta
    cavatappi, 110
    cooking, 37
    gnocchi, 137, 138
    orzo, 192

Pastry, 195
Pâte á Choux, 138
Pâte Sucrée, 195
Peaches, 140
Peacock, Thomas Love, 33
Peanut Butter & Jelly, 101
Pears
    compote, 39, 76
Peas, 137
Peppers
    ancho, 23
    arbol, 134
    braise, 23
    Jeremy's Chipotle
        Mayonnaise, 159
    New Mexico, 23
    serrano, 21
    toasting, 23
Pesto, 190
Peterson, James, 99
Pheasant
    hanging, 59
    spread, 60
Pistachios, 63
Plate Theory, 196
Plating, 68, 81
Plums
    pudding, 72, 73
    with quail, 120
    stewed, 49
Poële, 58
Point, Fernand, 56, 104
Polenta, 120
Pomegranates, 63
Pomelo, 68
Pork
    hock, 108
    pancetta, 157, 188
    pig trotters, 104
    sausage stuffing, 129
Potatoes
    in braise, 112
    cooking, 37, 86, 126
    fingerling, 36
    mashed, 104
    new, 126
    purée, 84
    Swedish Peanut, 145

Purslane, 182
La Pyramide, 56

Quail
    roast, 120
Question Authority, 183
Quietly Over Tea, 147

Radicchio, 192
Radishes
    French Breakfast, 143, 179
    Icicle, 179
    Red, 179
Raisins, 112
Ramps
    pickled, 134
Reducing, 34
Resting, 97
Rhubarb, 195
Rice
    Carolina Gold, 152
    Charleston "Ice Cream"
    Warm Indian Creamed Rice, 53
Robochon, Joel, 95
Rochat, Andre, 14, 159, 204
Root Vegetables
    preparing, 55
    in ragout, 34, 110
Roux, 95

Saffron
    in vinaigrette, 184
    cultivation of, 185
Saint Euphrosynus, 198
*Saint Euphrosynus, Patron Saint of
        Cooks, 199*
Salads
    assembling, 157
    Butter Crunch, Flame, and Paris
        White Lettuces, 143
    Cauliflower, 58
    dressing, 135
    Mache, Pomelo and Christmas
        Cactus Flower, 68

Orzo, Radicchio, Chick Pea and
    Herb Salad, 192
Roasted Beets, Beet Greens and
    Tatsoi with Freshly Grated
    Ginger and Chives, 44
Tatsoi and Sorrel with Pickled
    Ramps, Boiled Eggs and
    Tarragon, 134
Tender Greens, Crispy Capers,
    Pancetta and Almonds, 157
Updated Waldorf , 200
Warm Cactus and Chorizo, 21

Salt
cooking with, 37
Fleur de Sel, 126
and oil, 184
seasoning with, 203

Sauce
bread, 58
broken, 159, 179, 180
reducing, 34
velouté, 78
Saveur, 174
Seasoning, 203, 206
Side Dishes and Appetizers
Braised Winter Greens, 98
Buttermilk Biscuits with Bacon and
    Cheddar Cheese, 99
Charleston "Ice Cream," 152
Eggplant Caviar with Zucchini
    Sauce, 168
Foie Gras in Brioche with Pear
    Compote, 76

Goat Cheese Gnocchi, 137
Grilled Figs Wrapped in
    Pancetta, 188
Mashed Potatoes, 104
Moong Daahl with Early Snowball
    Cauliflower and Bloomsdale
    Long-Standing Spinach, 149
Mussels with White Beans, Kale,
    and Garlic, 32
New Potatoes and White
    Anchovies with Vinegar
    Onions, 126
Porcini Mushrooms and Fava
    Beans, 129
Purslane with Baby Beets, Braised
    Beet Greens, and Bacon, 182
Sautéed Walleye with Great
    Lakes Caviar and Champagne
    Sauce, 80
Smoked Whitefish with Onion
    Purée and Pea Shoots, 180
Simplicity, 56, 62, 81
Sisyphus and the Cook, 83
Sorrel, 134
Soups
    Artichoke with Walnuts and
        Parsley, 43
    Charentais Melon with
        Homemade Yogurt and
        Mint, 153
    Chestnut and Oyster Stew, 67
    Classic French Onion
        Gratinée, 94
    Mussel, White Bean, Kale and
        Garlic, 32
    Purée of Jerusalem Artichoke
        with Garlic Confit, 119
    Ragout of Root Vegetables and
        Mushrooms, 34
    Stinging Nettle with Horseradish
        Dumplings, 124
    Turnip with Turnip Greens and
        Bacon, 55
    Velouté of Sunchokes with
        Hazelnuts and Parsley, 78

Spices
    toasting, 157
Spinach,
    in curry, 149
    with halibut, 184
Stapelton, Olaf, 69
Star Anise, 84
Stews, 103
Stinging Nettles
    soup, 124
Stock
    chicken, 34,
    fond, 97
    recipe 113
Strawberries
    in red wine, 186
Sugar
    brown, 122
    caramel, 29
    cooking with, 28
Sunchokes
    origin of, 78
    purée, 119
    velouté, 78
Sweating, 37

Tangerines, 132
*The Taoist Tale of the Taming
        of the Harp, 48*
Tart Tatin, 204
Taste, 206
Tatin, Stephanie, 204
Tatsoi
    in salad, 44, 134
Tea
    bags, 122
    The Book of Tea, 48, 111
    Earl Grey Ice Cream, 122
    My Country and My People, 147
Temperatures, 36
Tempura, 143
Thich, Nhat Hanh, 53
Tillich, Paul, 139, 199
The Today Show, 153

Today's Quiet Repose, 111
Tomatoes, 23
Topolobampo, 23
Tortillas, 27
Troigras, 134
Troparian, 198
Turnips
    in braise, 202
    greens, 55
    roasted, 71
    soup, 55

An Unmeasured Life, 40

Van Dyke, Henry, 116
Vanilla
    extract, 175
    pod in sugar, 186
Vegetables
    cooking, 130
Velouté, 78
Venison, 104
Vinaigrette
    Cucumber-Saffron, 184
    Honey, 192
Vintage Poetry, 33

Waiters, 177
Wandering the Ventures of the Past, 69
Watercress, 58
Wine
    Barolo, 110
    Bordeaux, 60, 110
    Brunello, 110
    Cabernet Sauvignon, 84
    Champagne, 39
        sauce, 80
    Chardonnay, 34
    Chenin Blanc, 32
    Côtes du Rhône, 110
    cooking with, 80, 104, 202
    Ice, 39

Muscat, 49, 140
    pairing with food, 31, 32
    Pinot Noir, 36
    Port, 100
    Rhone, 60
    Riesling, 32
    Rosé, 34
    Sauternes, 39
    Sauvignon Blanc, 34
    Shiraz, 36
    Sparkling, 39
    Syrah, 60
    Zinfandel, 36
Wheeler, Mimi, 88
White, Marco-Pierre, 12, 83

Yellow on Yellow on Yellow on White, 56
Yogurt, 153

Zucchini, 168

acknowledgments

We would like to thank the following people who make our life possible:
Our amazing staff, who with total dedication help keep us on
the right track. The farmers and producers who call Michigan home.
Matt and Victoria Sutherland, who believed in us enough to publish
this book. Tom Kachadurian, whose photos illuminate our food.
To Sandra Salamony, who made our work both beautiful and legible.
To Chef Nancy Krcek Allen for her close reading of the original recipes,
and Heather Shaw, who with eternal patience took us by the hand and
helped us through every stage of writing this book. Finally, thanks to
John Blakeslee for all of his sage advice and wisdom.

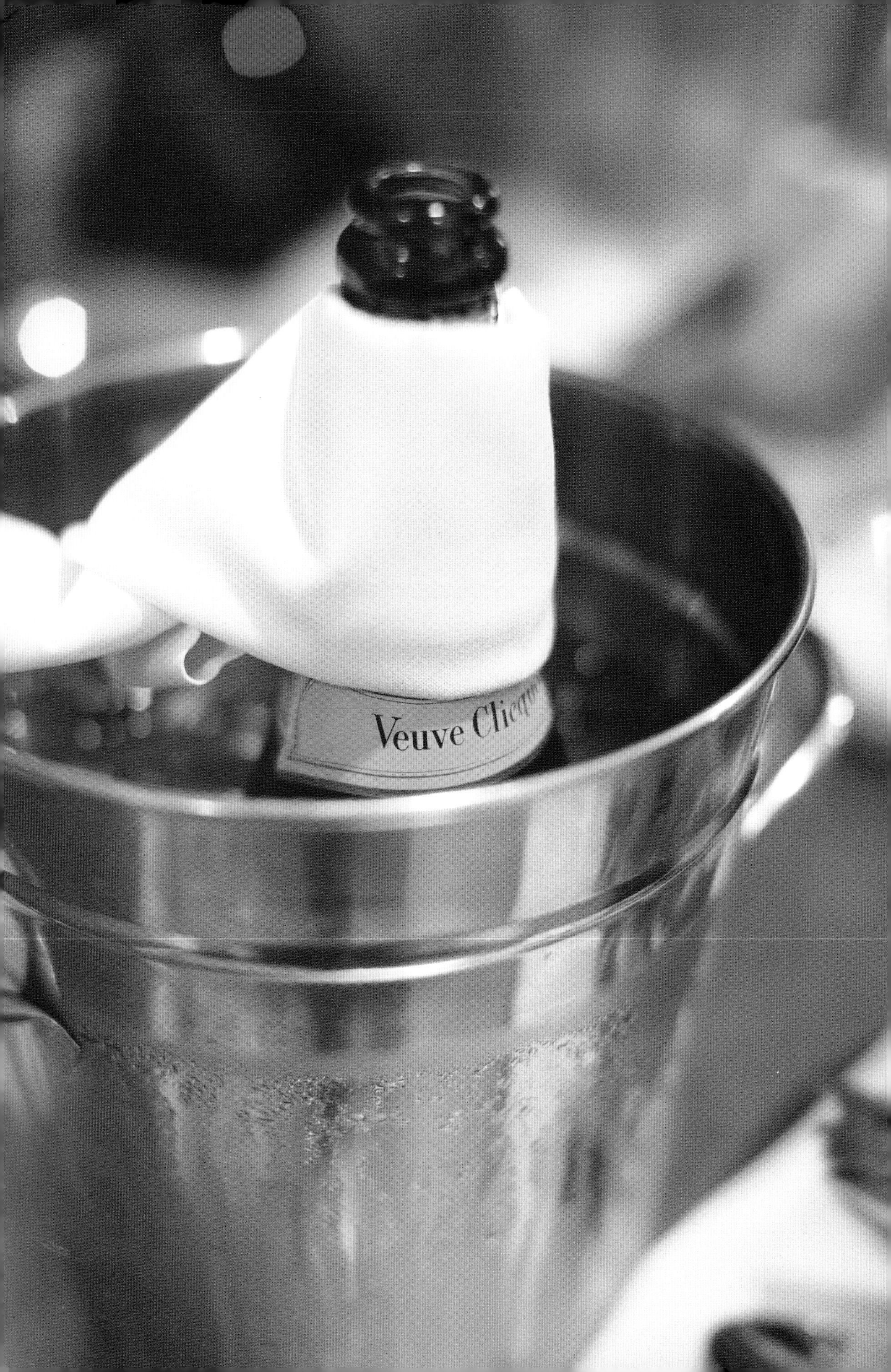
Veuve Clicq